Prescription for Youth

Maxwell Maltz

© Maxwell Maltz

© Copyright 2007 – BN Publishing

www.bnpublishing.com

info@bnpublishing.com

ISBN 956-291-432-1

Prescription for Youth

Contents

To Tobey and Joseph

The events described in this book are true, but in many cases fictitious names have been used.

The Question that Started this Book

I N ATTEMPTING TO HELP SOMEONE ELSE, IT OFTEN TURNS OUT that actually you are helping yourself. So at any rate with this book. It grew out of an interview I had one afternoon with a young man who had asked for my advice.

The young man's father, who is a doctor, had called me the day before. "You remember my boy Larry, don't you, Max?" he had asked.

"Yes, of course," I said.

"He wants to become a plastic surgeon, and he asked me to see if you'd mind giving him some general advice about it— if you were starting out, as he is now, what you'd do over again, what you wouldn't, and so on."

It is pleasant to be asked to dispense words of wisdom; not until later do you reflect that it may be difficult to find any to dispense. But after some anxious digging as the hour set for Larry to call on me approached, I found several things I could tell him that I thought would be of some benefit. For instance: in my time, the young man who aspired to a career in plastic surgery found it essential to go abroad to study. That was no longer necessary, thanks to great advances in the field in America. To-day, you were much more likely to find students coming here from all over the world.

Larry arrived within a minute of the appointed time, a sturdy young man with candid eyes and a slow, friendly smile. I need not have concerned myself about what advice I might find to give him; he had prepared himself thoroughly for the

9

interview with a list of questions, all of which were sensible and to the point.

The last one, though, stumped me.

It began innocently enough. "Dad says you've been in practice about twenty-five years, Doctor," Larry said. "You must have had lots of interesting patients. What would you say is the one thing of greatest value you've learned from them?"

The one thing of greatest value I had learned from my patients? This was a crusher. Of course, there were several stock answers I could give. Always keep your temper. Always be hopeful and cheerful. Never worry. But this young man with the frank, level eyes would know that they were merely parroted.

"I'm afraid it would take me a long time to figure that out, Larry," I said.

"I guess it was a pretty foolish question," he said. "Please, just forget it." And a little while later, after thanking me, he took his leave.

But I couldn't forget that question.

The one thing of greatest value I'd learned. . . .

That night I went out on the terrace, lit my pipe, and turned my mind back over the years—back much more than twenty-five years, back to the very beginning, old Attorney Street on New York's lower East Side. Of all the people you've known, I asked myself—not only patients—who are the ones who stand out in your memory?

After a while I got out pencil and paper, and wrote down a number of names and some notes:

Wingy. The beer wagon accident. The extraordinary right
   arm.
Mickey Henry, fellow-student at Columbia.
Carl Borger, M.D. The torture-chamber telephone booth.

Mr. Russell, and the case of the "African bug."

Kirillovna. The non-burning cigarette.

Ilsa Marisius. "In this slaughterhouse of a country, why must I alone be denied death?"

Caroline Nesbitt, who was astonished to find herself in New York.

The beautiful woman in Nicaragua who followed us from hospital to hospital.

The Ugly Duchess, and how and where we found her.

The young man in the bishop's palace at Ischia.

The mysterious traveller, that immaculate, old-fashioned gentleman.

Hercules and the geysers.

Mollie and the wonderful hat.

Frank Gordon and the doll that talked.

James Boysland, M.D.

For another hour or two I sat studying this list. Now, why had these people grouped themselves together in my mind?—for I had known others, patients as well as friends or acquaintances, who in many respects were more remarkable and who surely should have come into my mind first. But the question I had started with—Larry's question—was, What is the one thing of greatest value you've learned?—and, very dimly to begin with, the realization dawned on me that this group, taken all together, had taught me exactly that: the one thing of greatest value I had learned.

Each of these people constituted *one facet* of an answer to an old, old problem. That was the cord that bound them together, so that, remembering Wingy, the first on the list, I was bound to think next of Mickey Henry; and after Mickey, Dr. Borger; and so on down to the last.

The old, old problem, of course, was: *How to stay young.*

I say "of course" because the problem of staying young is one that the plastic surgeon is intimately familiar with; its physical aspect presents itself to him every day. When he is young, he may begin to think that the magic power of conquering time has been given to his fingers, as he sees them erase the sagging flesh of age; and in a measure this is so. But then he realizes that the power of his surgeon's knife is puny, for he sees (as I saw, in the case of Mr. Russell) a young man turned old almost overnight—and, incredibly, turned young again; a woman who according to every reasonable medical law should have been dead as a herring but who instead was vigorously alive and apparently imperishably youthful; and he marvels at the mystery and wonders what the answer is.

Perhaps if I wrote down all that I remembered about each of my fifteen people, some at least of that answer might come clear. At any rate, I resolved that it would do no harm to try.

So it was Larry's question, really, that led to this book.

The Kid with the Wing-Shaped Arm

WINGY IS THE FIRST PERSON WHO CAME TO MY MIND THAT evening—the first facet of the answer to the old problem of how to stay young. But before Wingy comes on to the scene, something should be said about that scene itself, as I remember it.

If you burrow through the tangle of Manhattan's lower East Side, eventually you will find Attorney Street, a midget lane leading into the great busy flow of Delancey Street. Back in the early 1900's, when I was a boy, Attorney Street and its neighbours constituted a kind of delicious jungle, boiling with life, where anything at all might happen.

We, the boys of my gang, were convinced that Attorney Street boasted that name because at one corner a bold gilt sign stared at you that said A. Poliakoff, Attorney. It followed that Mr. Poliakoff, despite his runty body and bowed legs and thick glasses, which gave the watery eyes a swollen, goldfishy kind of look, was a person to respect; for how many people are there in this world powerful and important enough to have streets named after them?

We were only dimly aware of the mighty surrounding empire of Manhattan. The towers of the downtown business section looked much the same to us as the distant lordly Himalayas must look to the villagers of the Indian plain. In a sense we were both big city boys and small town boys at the same time; the rumble and grime of the metropolis filled the air, and yet Tom Sawyer would have needed no more than a glance to recognize us as brothers under the skin.

He had the Mississippi; we, the East River. Nobody bothered about filth and bacteria then; even if they had, would we have heeded them? Keep us out of that bountiful paradise, that pool of rare delights? How wonderful, on a steaming summer day, to plunge down from the wharf into the dappled dark-green water and come up sputtering and tingling to see some great ship slowly swimming up the tide!—the splendour and magnificence of which was of course often balanced by the remains of ancient oranges and melons slowly swimming down.

Tom Sawyer had his Indian cave; we had the crumbling warehouses on the waterfront and deserted tenements far gone in decay. When you stepped inside the sagging doorway the gloom wrapped around you like a cloak and it required small effort to fancy yourself a mile underground, with only the bones of ancient Indian warriors to keep you company. The dank, sad air was spiced by danger; at any moment the creaking floor might collapse and send you hurtling into the abyss.

Life on Attorney Street was most exciting on election nights and when saint days came along, as they did (it seems to me now) in profusion. If it was a dingy local contest or the Presidency itself, our enthusiastic patriotism differed not a whit; the event had to be celebrated in bang-up style, and for days beforehand we scrounged the neighbourhood in search of food for the great joyous election night bonfires.

The saint days came into their real glory at night too; then old Attorney Street became a gorgeous Oriental wonderland of sputtering lights and ribbons and flowers and flags and music, wonderful music, music that marched into your blood and set your heels drumming in rapture. There would be booths for games of chance in which you tried to toss pennies into a pot or guessed on a turn of the cards or threw balls at rubber cats, and pushcarts lined up in long steaming rows for the vendors of hot meats and fish and pizzas and spaghetti and clams and richly coloured candies, monstrously appealing in their dripping goo—and franks, of course, glorious frankfurters, smothered in the fragrant kraut.

And all the time the brave brass band would attend gallantly to its business, oomphing and poomphing away steadily, big fat red-faced moustached men all of them, no lightweights here, none of your fragile uptown violinists but champion blowers who could blast good solid music at you for an hour or more and hardly pause for breath and engulf a quart of beer as coolly and nonchalantly as you would take a sip of water, and think nothing of it, and return to blowing like elephants refreshed.

In the midst of this carnival of noise and sweat and smell, suddenly you would stumble on the flower-crowned shrine of the saint, an oasis of silence. Dark forms bowed before the blandly smiling figure; a filigree of dollar bills pinned around its bower demonstrated their zeal.

On these gala nights we all had enough to eat, an achievement that some of us could never exactly manage at home. After washing up and stowing away their paraphernalia, the pushcart vendors would distribute any left-over perishables among us. What extraordinary mixtures we ate then! What extraordinary dreams we had!

In the morning, as if it had all been only a dream too, wonderland had vanished; Attorney Street was again the same old patchwork quilt of scabby storefront, rusty fire escape and stained cement, the housewives back in the tenement windows, elbows rooted in a pillow, brooding over the busy street, occasionally shouting gossip across thirty feet of space with such vehemence that the pigeons would scatter in alarm from the rooftops above, or hauling back some mischief-bound kid with the lariat of their powerful voices.

One of those kids was Wingy.

Wingy was the president of our gang (other gangs had chiefs or leaders; we were different; we modelled ourselves strictly on the political set-up of the U.S.A.). The astonishing thing about this was that Wingy wasn't a boy, she was a girl.

Certainly you would have been hard put to it to recognize
the fact, seeing Wingy in her raggedy cropped-off boy's pants,
her old greenish-brown sweater and scuffed sneakers, her hair
tucked up under a hat so ancient, so frankly deplorable and
dispirited that even we, well accustomed to hopeless, battered
inheritances from older members of the family, wondered why
Wingy clung to it. No, you would never have taken her for
a girl, except perhaps when she smiled.

There had been no smiling on Wingy's part until a few
months before she was elected our president. But no reasonable person would have wondered why the thin face with the
large thoughtful eyes was so solemn; she carried the explanation
around with her, dangling at her side. It explained her name,
too. Her right arm was crooked out from the shoulder in such
a way that the upper arm continued the horizontal shoulder
line; but the lower arm was notched down sharply, bent in at
a sudden angle so that the hand pointed approximately to
Wingy's waist. The whole formed a kind of V. The V could
be swung back and forth, the fingers could be used to grasp
and hold small articles, but the arm could not be unfolded. It
flapped when she ran, and that was how Wingy earned her
name; the arm looked like the wing of a bird in flight.

This V-shaped arm was born in an accident. Our jungle
streets on the lower East Side clattered with a great slow
lumbering tide of wagons and drays. The mightier of these
carts offered much sport. They moved slowly; and we, nimble
on our feet, quick as cats, would dodge in and out between
the huge groaning wheels. It only added to the charm of this
cobblestone ballet that the teamster might flick his snake-
tongue lash out after your moving behind and excise a spot of
hide; these were honourable scars, to be paraded and boasted
about.

A hearty masculine game. It offended us to see Wingy take
part in it (of course she was not called Wingy then; she was
plain Mary Elizabeth O'Reilly), and we predicted that this

brash female, who insisted on trying to join us instead of staying with the girls where she belonged, would come to grief.
As she did; but it was due to no lack of skill or nimbleness on
her part.

Darting underneath a massive wagon pyramided high with
beer barrels, she had the misfortune to encounter on that
perilous territory a small animal bound in the opposite direction. This small yellow dog was living in a nightmare and
proclaiming his terror to the indifferent world. For somebody
had tied a string of cans to his tail and added a dollop of turpen-
tine to a spot just beneath his tail to speed him on his way.

Though others paid no attention to him, the horses hauling
the beer wagon heard his voice all too keenly and became
alarmed; they reared back, then lunged ahead, thus upsetting
Wingy's precise calculations with respect to the great slow-
turning wheels. The wheels accelerated suddenly; in that
instant Wingy was knocked from her feet; and, tumbling head
over heels, her right arm became caught between two spokes
of the right rear wheel.

Those who saw the accident could not understand why her
arm was not torn off. Wingy and her parents were informed
that there could not be a more fortunate child in the world.
For a long time Wingy hardly thought so. The effect of the
accident was to freeze the arm in the peculiar, grotesque V-
shape. Orthopædic surgery might have undone the damage
but only in a series of operations; and who was going to
arrange a series of operations for Mary Elizabeth O'Reilly, the
eighth and youngest child of the O'Reillys of Attorney Street?

So Mary Elizabeth found herself in possession of a new arm
and a new name. The latter was given to her the first time she
went flapping down Attorney Street. "Hey, lookit," said
somebody or other. "Wingy!"

Never a social success, Wingy was now treated like a leper.
We wished to have her around us less than ever: she was not
only a girl, she had become a kind of freak too.

There seemed to be nothing left for her to do, even though the summer, the best time of the whole year, was just beginning. To dive into the East River with her new arm would be like tying herself to an anchor. No swimming. Nothing to do but sit and stare at life. But Wingy was no one to sit still; instead she took to going off on long lonely hikes up and down the Manhattan perimeter.

Thus Wingy met a new—and one-armed—career.

The waterfront is a fascinating land; the docks are good to look at and good to smell; you can smell your way around the world there in half an hour of sniffing. You may not associate each smell accurately with its native land but your common sense tells you these smells are not domestic smells; they are the smells of spices and hides and coconuts and a thousand and one exotic stuffs packed across the seven seas in a deep ship belly to be unloaded before your very eye and nose on a New York wharf. There is a happy tribe of people so blessed by fortune that their official estate in life is to live among these smells. They are known as longshoremen.

Longshoremen are not only provided with this delicious diet of smells and the sight of the great foreign ships nuzzling to wharfside and lying obediently idle while their holds are stripped, they are given a tool more romantic than cavalry sabre or Gurkha kukri with which to work—a hook, a real hook of steel, wicked, rounded and gleaming. This hook they hold in their right hand and whack into the midriff of the perfumed bales, meanwhile swearing wonderfully out of pure happiness.

By the hour Wingy would stand on this wharf or that, smelling the smells and admiring the men as their hooks flashed in the summer sun.

But Pier Number 42, East River, became her favourite. For a particularly gifted hook artist operated there, a gigantic man who swore like a poet and sweated supremely. One day he noticed his small audience and, like any nobleman, bowed to

it. "Whatcha say, kid?" he inquired, flinging off gallons of
sweat in a diamond rainfall. "You want anything?"

Wingy found herself bold enough to speak. "I wish I could
help," she said.

"Wish you could *help*?" the large man repeated, but he
didn't laugh. Instead he looked at Wingy more carefully.
"What's wrong with your arm?" he asked.

Wingy explained about the beer wagon.

"What were you doing under a beer wagon?"

"It was a game," Wingy said. "All the boys played it. Running under the wagon and——but I got caught."

The large man knelt and touched the arm cautiously. "You
can't move it no more than this?" he said in a subdued voice.
"Just this little bit?"

Well, no, she couldn't, Wingy was forced to admit. "But,"
she added, "my left arm's fine."

"What's your name, kid?"

"Mary Elizabeth O'Reilly. Though lately," she said, "since
this happened, they've been calling me Wingy."

"You telling me you're a *girl*?"

"But I thought you knew!" Wingy cried despairingly.

"With them clothes you're wearing?"

The large man had now assumed a complexion roughly
purple in hue. At length sound issued from him, like a geyser,
relieving his cheeks of their awful blush; but Wingy could not
be sure if the sound was anger or what.

"Wait here, Mary Elizabeth," the large man instructed her,
and he rejoined his fellows. Soon, in a group, they came over
to her.

"What give you the notion you want to work here, Mary
Elizabeth?" one of them asked.

"I know how it looks and smells," Wingy informed him.
"And I'd like to grow up to be someone like all of you."

"Ain't there something else you ought to be doing, with
your ma or someone?"

"She's just as glad when I'm not at home," Wingy said.

"All right, Mary Elizabeth," he said. "You're hired."

She was not, however, given a hook, but it would have been sheer madness and folly to dream that she might be. Already she had leaped into a position so superb she marvelled at her luck. In this glorious leap she had become General Assistant, Pier Number 42, East River, in which capacity she served chiefly as a hauler and runner: she hauled the water bucket to and fro, and fetched necessary items of equipment, and ran to get the beer growlers filled at lunch time. The flapping right arm rowed her up and down the pier while the fine left arm worked prodigiously.

It was a wonderful summer.

She rose in the pearly, hushed early morning light and reported for work at half past seven. Toil continued without let-up until the lunch hour. In the beginning Wingy ate chastely of the few items her mother's poor kitchen provided, which sometimes amounted to nothing at all except a bracing glass of water. She had a favourite place to sit for lunch, commanding the best view of the East River with its fishing gulls and steady procession of ships and barges; but one day she found her seat already occupied. The intruder was a huge corned beef sandwich, so imposing in girth that she feared it had got there by mistake. Puzzled, she looked around. Her original friend, the large man who had first addressed her, met her eye somewhat furtively. "Go ahead," he said through his mouthful of food, which, curiously, was corned beef too. "You work hard, you got to eat."

Every day now vast slabs of meat and spectacular carvings of bread, with onions and apples tastefully attached, joined her for lunch. That was not all she received. The head longshoreman gravely explained that longshoremen all over the world held it as a cardinal principle of their faith that no longshoreman however humble should labour without being paid. In other words, she, Mary Elizabeth, being now a sort of junior longshoreman, or perhaps he should say, longshoregirl, must accept at the end of each week a certain sum in return for her runnings and haulings, or be dismissed instantly.

Thus, she was fed, and she was paid.

But finally that long, wonderful summer came to an end at last and the jaws of school opened again. After school, Wingy still repaired to her pier and her working associates. She had been with them for nearly four months now; they had seen her every day with the exception of Sundays, and so they realized only vaguely that certain changes in her had occurred. Wingy realized it even less; and as for the rest of us kids, not at all.

In the last week of October, Indian summer suddenly bloomed. The heat was gorgeous. Back we ran to the East River for the bathing pleasures we had thought were finished for another long weary winter and spring.

A dropsical family of sand barges had tied up around the wharf we regarded as our own; they mumbled and grumbled gently as their shaggy wooden hides chafed against the pilings and occasionally uttered the long despairing sigh produced by a hawser pulled tight by the impulse of the outgoing tide below. These behemoths were no strangers to us; we knew them intimately, from earlier visits. On the stern of each barge sat its skipper's snug little shanty, where he (more caretaker than navigator) had his stove and his bunk and his companion dog or cat, usually a character of sour disposition too.

One could hardly blame these barge men for their evil tempers; the life of an ocean-going janitor is an excruciatingly boring business: he has absolutely no social standing and is perhaps more thoroughly unappreciated than any other variety of mariner. Small wonder that during his stays in port he will seize every opportunity to vanish into the nearest grog shop, where all men are equal, or reasonably so.

It was this fact alone that made it possible for us to enjoy ourselves on the sand barges. To-day, the caretaker dogs had left with their caretaker masters; only one ancient cat brooded inscrutably over the scene. She was soon taken into custody and after an athletic half hour departed vigorously for regions unknown. Now we were monarchs of all we surveyed.

What we surveyed was a mountain range of clean sand, soft to the seat and perfect for burrowing. While some of us dug tunnels, others constructed a long slide down one mountain flank. You slithered down this sand slide and catapulted into the water, then swam around the barge to the wooden cleats nailed to one of the wharf pilings, and so up to the barge for a repeat performance.

At length, inevitably, sliders and tunnel diggers united activities in one game, a magnificent form of King of the Mountain, magnificent in that losing possession of the peak was a pleasure, since the East River awaited you below. We kept at it until the early fall shadows began climbing down from inside the tenements and lofts and reaching out for us on the barge. It began to be difficult to see what you were doing. But still there was an almost noontime heat and no one wanted to leave.

We were all very sandy and very noisy and somewhat confused by natural exhaustion and the dim light, and a good ten minutes must have gone by before we realized that one of the noises mixing in the general uproar over the sand barge was a yell of pain and terror. When we traced it to its source we discovered that a recent King of the Mountain, Red Schapps, noted for his carrot hair and big feet, had not fallen into the water after his dethronement but had inadvertently tumbled the other way and in consequence now lay wedged between the side of the barge and the side of the pier.

Red was a clumsy fellow, always getting into some kind of fix, and at first we thought his predicament merely funny. He corrected us. He was scared out of his wits. His foot was trapped and he could not pull it loose and it was beginning to hurt. The barge had several hundred tons of sand in its belly and was slow to move but if wind or tide swung it in another inch or two against the pier Red's foot would be crushed and perhaps his leg and perhaps, eventually, all of him.

We began to try to get Red out. The trouble was, he was situated so awkwardly that only one of us at a time could reach him. Soon his terror infected all of us and we became silly and ineffectual, wasting our strength in shouted directions and stupid advice. Red's usually pink and good-natured face was a pale tear-wet blob in the dusk and the noises he made sounded like a baby's. Finally someone found enough sense go to running for a cop or anyway someone grown-up and strong enough to pull Red loose.

But instead, after a few minutes what we saw running towards us along the wharf was the ridiculous and familiar figure of Wingy, rowing the air with her right arm as she always did when she ran. Having finished her afternoon's work, she had been coming home along the waterfront when the messenger sent for help had bolted past her, yelling out in answer to her question what was wrong: "Red's stuck up there!"

We told Wingy to beat it but she pushed through us brusquely. She knelt at the edge of the pier, located Red, and reached her left arm, the good arm, down to him. "Take hold of me," she said, and Red did so. Wingy pulled, and up he came.

For some time, quite naturally, there was a period of shock: the impossible had happened before our eyes and no one could believe it. Except Red. He was crouched on the pier, massaging his bruised foot. He couldn't speak yet, but when he looked up the smile he gave Wingy was a pretty good one.

With all the use to which Wingy had put that left arm of hers on the pier with her longshoremen friends, it had grown very strong indeed.

But Mary Elizabeth O'Reilly didn't grow up to be a longshoreman, her stated ambition that summer when she had been a lonely, unwanted, crippled small girl. Eventually, through a combination of efforts, the V-shaped right arm was repaired by surgery; and some time after that—a couple of years, as I remember it now—Mary Elizabeth resigned the presidency of our gang (to which we had elected her following her rescue of Red) and turned into a girl and then into a young woman; and before very long she was married and beginning a family of her own.

There is nothing unusual here; it is the predictable future of most tomboys. The unusual thing is that, by refusing to let the handicap of a crippled arm reduce her life to one of withdrawal and useless brooding over her lot, Mary Elizabeth all unwittingly acquired a strength she had never had before.

And that, of course, was why I remembered her. Not so much because of the dramatic rescue but because of her stubborn refusal to quit. Wingy was someone who, whatever the circumstances, would *keep going*, and whose heart therefore would remain forever young.

Mickey Was All Set to Die
When He Found a Letter

ANY CLASS OF MEDICAL STUDENTS IS BOUND TO CONTAIN A "character" or two. Perhaps the most colourful in our class of 1923 at the College of Physicians and Surgeons of Columbia University was Barney Auer.

Barney owned an infinite fertility of invention and believed heart and soul that there was a way round anything. Well, almost anything. He admitted that the orthodox Jewish ban on smoking—and practically anything else—during the Sabbath had him stumped. He was the faithful son of highly orthodox parents and would not think of disobeying them. A confirmed chain smoker, his Sabbath day sufferings were frightful to behold. He paced like a caged lion; his usual whimsical, rather cockeyed expression changed into horrible scowls, while he muttered unpleasant words under his breath and rapidly consumed liquorice drops.

Rather than subject himself to this ordeal every seventh day, I suggested, why not take the plunge and give up smoking altogether? It would be grim for a while but by and by, think what he would gain!

"Nonsense, man," said Barney contemptuously, pausing and striking a clenched hand against his forehead. "I tell you there is an answer to this, there is, there is. I feel it in my bones."

I well remember the day he found the answer. It was one Sabbath morning and I was sleeping the sleep of the utterly

25

worn out. Already, at five or six o'clock, poor Barney must have been rooted out of bed by the private devil that would not let him sleep every seventh morning but insisted on starting his sufferings early. Presently a knock on my door proved that this was indeed so. Soon the knocker scorned further knocking and opened the door without being invited to. There stood Barney, with a radiant look on his face.

"Get up, man, get up!" he chanted. "Rise, and give thanks! The day of deliverance has come!—providing, that is," he added, running forward, kneeling beside my bed, pulling me over and gazing anxiously into my face, "—providing that your people have no objections to smoking on the Sabbath?"

"What are you talking about?" I said in the feeble voice of the ex-sleeper only half awake.

"Have they?"

"Have they what?"

"Have they any objections to your smoking on the Sabbath?"

"No, they haven't," I said. "What about it?"

"Glory, glory!" Barney shouted. "Up, man, up! No more talk—forward!" And he hoisted me from the bed and stood me on my feet.

At once his face fell. Barney was a couple of inches over six feet in height. The top of my head just about came to his chin. He eyed me gloomily, then sat me down on the edge of the bed and seated himself alongside. Here we were much on a level; the difference between us when standing was due chiefly to his extremely long legs. Cheering up, he reached around and pulled the window wide open and a brisk breeze came flowing into the room. Barney regarded the flapping curtains with approval, then put his hand into his pocket and drew out a plump new package of cigarettes.

"Have one," he said cordially.

"No thank you," I said.

"Max," he said, even more warmly, "have one!"

"But I don't want one," I protested. "You know I'm not much of a smoker, and this early in the morning I just don't feel——"

A glint that I knew well appeared in Barney's eye. "Max," he declared, "this is no laughing matter." Neither of us was laughing. "I am asking you politely and equably, with the affection and esteem of long friendship, to accept a cigarette. Not just any cigarette, but a delicious Murad. Surely the least you can do is not to quibble but to respond with the proper appreciation, as a friend should?"

"Oh, all right," I grumbled, and took the cigarette. Barney lit it for me, with what I can only describe as motherly care.

"Delicious, isn't it?" he inquired. "Take a big mouthful. Go on, don't be bashful—a big, big one. Don't bother to inhale. All right?"

I nodded.

"Good," Barney said. "So now, blow it at me as hard as you can!"

And he leaned forward with a beatific smile.

For one cannot properly be said to smoke, he maintained, unless one holds, ignites and draws from the cigarette all by oneself. If one's mouth should happen to be open at the instant one's neighbour happens to expel a cloud of smoke into the breeze that happens to be blowing towards one, and if through this combination of circumstances the smoke should enter one's mouth so vigorously as to penetrate to one's lungs, can this properly be called smoking? Moses himself would not have said so.

If Barney was the most colourful member of our class, certainly the most popular was Mary James. She was so pretty that none of us ever thought she would actually take her degree. Somebody would be bound to marry her first. And then, there was the famous incident of the dissecting room, which did not really happen in the room itself but on its threshold.

In those years the college's dissecting room was on the top floor of the Vanderbilt Building. You got to it not by an interior but exterior staircase that ran up the outside of the building like a fire escape, very steep and narrow. On the day when we were first introduced to the dissecting room Mary James was leading the line of students climbing these stairs. Of course she knew where we were headed but she couldn't have thought much about it; a good-looking college girl is inclined to live pretty much in the moment, never look very far ahead—at least so it seemed to me, observing Mary and the stir of courtship always going on around her.

So when Mary arrived at the top of the stairs she was not really prepared for what lay ahead. She had been chattering away gaily in the bright sunshine, and now suddenly a cloud seemed to crawl over the sun, while an evil smell, intimating much, and all of it very unpleasant, invaded her nostrils. Mary took one look into the gloom across the threshold, saw the lines of cold pale cadavers, uttered a shriek and fell over backwards. We were packed close together behind her and under the impact about half of us went sprawling like a row of ninepins, right down the stairs.

Our professor informed us that this was the most dramatic reaction he had yet seen to the dissecting room; and he wondered audibly if Mary would be able to stand the rigours of the next three years. We wondered too. Definitely she seemed to be out of place.

The load of our studies piled up higher and higher as the term advanced. I couldn't remember when I'd last had an absolutely carefree Saturday and Sunday without anything to do. Saturdays were the worst. There were the endless medical books to read, there was the cigarette smoke to be blown at Barney, if I was so unfortunate as to be cornered and trapped by him. I was fond of Barney and could not very well spurn his piteous pleas to have mercy and blow Murads at him every

Saturday; moreover, he pointed out, think how cosy and convenient it was, sitting side by side, studying like true comrades-in-arms, each one helping the other over the tough spots. (It was impossible not to reflect that one of the comrades-in-arms seemed to be doing more of the helping over rough spots than the other.) I stoked myself with cigarettes and fumed like a volcano while Barney thrived and praised my brotherly spirit lavishly. But this chore had one beneficial effect on me; it caused me to loathe cigarettes so heartily I have never smoked them since.

In the midst of this dreary business an even drearier event took place. Our classmate Mickey Henry fell sick. At first he said it was nothing, only a cold—well, maybe a bad cold; the next thing we knew he was in the hospital and rapidly shooting downhill. At the very brink of the last black gulf he hesitated, hovered there agonizingly, and then seemed slowly to pull back, but only a very, very little. That was more or less the common history of influenza in those days before the great discoverers of the thirties and forties, Fleming and Waksman and the others, came in to step on its neck.

It was appalling to see the change wrought in Mickey by only a week or two. He had been as husky as a football star, a veritable Arrow collar ad type, blooming cheeks and curly blond hair and bright fresh friendly eyes. A grey hand seemed to have taken him in its grasp and squeezed him into a shell of his former self; even the blond hair seemed to have lost its colour and become sickly and washed-out looking, like old straw.

It was difficult to keep your spirits up and put on the proper show of good cheer when you went to see him. Those dull, leaden eyes gazed at you, you fancied, with envy and reproach; envy of your good health, reproach that you and all the world that had once been so friendly and so secure for Mickey Henry had somehow let this happen to him.

We all took turns visiting him, until that day when the grim little sign appeared on Mickey's door: NO VISITORS. I forget who discovered the sign; at any rate, we learned the reason wasn't because Mickey had taken a turn for the worse but simply because the visits of his friends and family seemed to have an effect quite the reverse of the intended one; they left him depressed, more lack-lustre than ever, more disinterested in life. So his doctor had decided to put him on the no-visiting for a while.

Had I been in Mickey's place, I remember thinking, I would have asked for this to be done. I wouldn't want anyone sitting at my bedside stumbling through the lame little jokes and grinning at me with determined brightness, pretending that everything was the same, everything was exactly the same, when we both knew so very well it wasn't. I would have wanted to kick everybody out, together with their pity that had brought them there.

And so Mickey was left alone. Once we had thought of him every day, because his visitor of the evening before had given us the latest news. Now, in only a few days, he was virtually forgotten. We couldn't help it. There was too much work to do; we were caught up and swept on by the all-demanding rush—the real world became unreal, even your parents seemed like strangers. The only reality lay in the everlasting books that you hauled home with you at night.

Then one afternoon when I was walking with Mary James to the subway, she said, quite out of the blue, "Mickey was asking for you yesterday—said to be sure to give you his regards."

"Mickey?" I repeated, thoroughly astonished. "You been seeing him? But I thought he was——"

"Oh, they took him off no visitors a few days ago. He's coming along wonderfully."

"Gosh, what happened?"

"I'm going down there to-night between seven and eight. Would you like to come along?"

30

"I certainly would," I said.

Mary and I met at the hospital a few minutes before seven. She had a load of text books in her arms. "For Mickey," she explained. "He's reading like mad to make up for lost time."

"Just between you and me," I said, "the last time I saw him, I thought—well, I thought——"

"I know," she said solemnly. "I thought so too."

Mickey was sitting up in bed. And it really was Mickey. Still rather pale and a good deal underweight, but the grey look was gone. He had been reading a book; when he glanced up and saw us he slapped it together with a bang and held out both his hands, taking one of Mary's and one of mine. "Sit down, folks, and eat, drink and be merry," he said in large, enthusiastic tones, indicating the baskets of fruit and boxes of candy. "Gee, is it good to see you!"

I could only marvel at him in silence. And he interpreted my silence correctly.

"I guess when you saw me last you never thought you would again, eh Maxie?"

"Oh, I wouldn't say that exactly," I protested.

"Not much you wouldn't say that exactly. You'd have said it too, wouldn't you, Mary?"

"You were terribly sick, Mickey," she began, "but——"

"Terribly sick all over," said Mickey with the same enthusiasm. "Up here too"—he tapped his head—"in the brain department."

"—but that's all finished now," Mary interrupted. "Before long you'll forget all about it."

"Sweet, pretty Mary," Mickey said, taking her hand again. "You don't know how wrong you are. There's one part of it I'm never going to forget. It's quite a story, at least I think so. Would you like to hear it?"

"We certainly would," I told him; and Mickey sat back against his pillows and began.

Apparently it all started on the day a little more than a

month before when the NO VISITORS sign had been put up on the door of Mickey's room.

"Listen, Doctor," Mickey had said that afternoon when the doctor had stepped in, "will you do something for me? Write down in the order book that I'm not to have any visitors for a while. Okay?"

"Now, that's an odd thing for a good-looking young fellow like you to be asking," said the doctor suavely. "What's the trouble?"

"I know they mean well," Mickey said, "but the truth is, I just seem to be knocked out by the time they leave. I guess I try to talk too much for my own good. Honest, I think it would help me along if you did as I say."

As a matter of fact, the doctor had been meditating some such step himself, for his patient had made no progress at all in the last week. "You're the doctor," he declared; at which Mickey laughed dutifully, thanked him, and then, when the older man had left, turned over in his bed with a sigh of relief.

He had not told the doctor the truth, for the excellent reason that he had known exactly what the doctor would say—"Now, now, my boy, *that's* not the way to feel! Merely an effect of what you've been through; you'll soon be over it, mark my words." The truth was not that his visitors tired him physically or that he tried to talk too much for his own good. No, his visitors didn't tire him, they irritated him. No, even that wasn't the truth.

The honest-to-God, rock-bottom truth was that he was bored with the whole bunch of them, bored with the way they looked, bored with the way they talked, bored with every single, solitary thing about them and the lives they led—his college friends and his family and his family's friends. Perhaps, as the doctor would surely have said had he been given the chance, perhaps this was only a lingering effect of the disease that had almost killed him; but Mickey didn't think so.

No, you couldn't shrug this thing off so simply. For Mickey had made a great discovery here in his hospital room. He had discovered the essential ridiculousness of life.

If only all these petty people—his friends and relatives—could see themselves as he saw them! If only they could see as clearly as he saw the monstrous farce their little lives made! But of course they couldn't; they were blind and stupid; they thought their toilings and scrabblings had vast importance; and he was bound here by the chains of his illness, forced to look at them and listen to them twice a day.

But no, there was a way to get rid of them after all; and the doctor fell for it.

So the door closed, and the NO VISITORS sign was put up. The only thing Mickey had to fear now was the day when he would be forced to return to that world outside, that ridiculous world of fools, barbarians and knaves. He felt that rather than be sentenced to the weary round of living day in and day out with his fellow Yahoos he would prefer to stay in this two-by-four hospital cubicle, where his solitude was disturbed only by the visits of the day and night nurses and, of course, the doctor.

The doctor bumbled away about how Mickey would soon be up and around again as good as new; but there was a secret knowledge growing now inside Mickey's head that permitted him to mock—oh, quite to himself, of course, while nodding his head gravely in apparent agreement—these optimistic medical statements. This secret knowledge was a lovely thing. It had really been there all the time, Mickey knew; he just somehow hadn't been lucky enough to hit on it before. It amounted to this: Don't worry about what the doctor says, don't worry about having to live again in that vulgar world outside the hospital walls; for if you wish hard enough never to return to it, why, you never will. You will stay here in your bed, drifting away as if in a dream, leaving all the rottenness behind.

One irritation remained: the nurses. The eight-to-four day-time nurse and the four-to-midnight nurse between them had to bring him his meals, change his bed, bathe him and give him his medicine and his evening alcohol rub. After the blissful experience of having no visitors had worn off somewhat, it began to seem to Mickey that the damned nurses were almost always in his room, bathing him or feeding him or fixing the bed. He wished there were some way of getting rid of them entirely, but of course that couldn't be done. At least he made it evident that he didn't like them, which cut their conversational exchanges down to the barest essentials.

Then one afternoon the day nurse made an unscheduled call, when she had no business being in his room. He looked up in annoyance. "I'm sorry, Mr. Henry," she said—ridiculous little woman she was, with one eye slightly off centre, which gave her a stupid wandering kind of look—"I didn't want to disturb you but I misplaced something and I thought—I mean, I wondered if by some chance I just happened to drop it when I was——" she was looking around busily as she spoke, with little pecking motions of her head, like a daft hen, "when I was fixing your bed."

"What was it?" Mickey asked.

"A letter."

"Haven't seen any letter," Mickey said. "You must have left it somewhere else."

"I suppose so. I'm sorry to have disturbed you, Mr. Henry."

"All right," Mickey said grumpily, and closed his eyes again.

Later in the afternoon, when the day nurse had left and the night nurse had come on for her shift, Mickey reached over to the utility table beside his bed for a glass of water and saw that a piece of paper had slipped down behind the table. He picked it up and unfolded it. It was a letter—obviously the day nurse's letter. Mickey had not the remotest glimmer of interest in her correspondence but no one not entirely moribund could have

refrained from finishing the letter after having read the saluta-
tion; for it began:

My Priceless Rapture:
Mickey read the rest of the letter.

All in all, it was pretty incredible. He read the letter several
times, more amazed each time. It got to be something like a
hideous chorus in his mind.

My Priceless Rapture [said this lunatic letter]:
*May I dare call you that? Pray permit me to, for 'twill be the
sweetest boon e'er granted mortal man. I have thought of you in such
terms, if truth be told, since the day when first my eyes met yours.
Twin oases of serene blue!—offering surcease and bliss to the weary
traveller!—ah, I bless those radiant eyes, and the cupid's arrow fired
from them that pierced my heart so surely!*

(God damn it, Mickey said to himself at this point on every
reading of the letter, God damn it, twin oases that fire arrows
yet!)

But e'en greater glories lie beneath those gorgeous cerulean pools
[the letter continued strongly]. *Your lips, fresh and ripe as red
rosebud petals. You must know, my darling inspiration, that there
lives no man who, after but one glance at those treasures, could refrain
from yearning to crush them 'neath the fevered impress of his own.
And so have I yearned—and so do I aspire.*

*Enough for now. May I continue to address you? You need send
but one word in reply to transport me to a paradise unimaginable.
That word—need I tell you?—is yes.*

Yours in adoration,
Geoffrey

Geoffrey, Mickey said to himself; Geoffrey, for Christ's sake!
I always thought Geoffrey wasn't a bad kind of name, by and
large, up to now; but from now on I'll never be able to see the

name Geoffrey without just slightly throwing up. Geoffrey, for God's sake; have they got you in a straitjacket yet, old man?

But after thinking about the incredible Geoffrey for some time and reading the letter once again, Mickey realized that it was even worse to think about the nurse whose letter this was. He tried to put her out of his mind but found he couldn't; he saw her as clearly as if she were in the room at this moment, hunting around for her maudlin letter, with her wandering eye and her foolish bewildered expression, pecking her head back and forth. The day nurse actually had received this letter, she actually had been carrying it around with her, it actually meant a lot to her—Geoffrey to her was not a fugitive from a nut house, no, no; Geoffrey in the day nurse's pathetic estimation was, obviously, a god who strode the earth, a lover to make Don Juan wince with envy.

Gee, Mickey thought, if he writes that kind of letter to her, I wonder what kind of letter *she* writes to *him*!

But it couldn't be true, he decided, scanning the impassioned prose again. There's no one nutty enough in this day and age to carry on like some character straight out of Edward Robert Bulwer-Lytton, Earl of Lytton, which as far as he remembered was the noble lord's interminable name. Still, there was the letter, written in purple ink on paper of excellent quality. Yours in adoration, Geoffrey.

Mickey folded the letter back into its original creases and put it away. His dreams that night were tinged with an impossible combination of blue oases shooting out fiery arrows while a Sir Galahad-like individual clad in Oscar Wilde-ish costume whirled around mincingly in the sky overhead like a crazy ballet dancer.

When the day nurse came in the next morning, Mickey looked at her with genuine curiosity. No, she had no charms that he could see to turn a man into an idiot; she was definitely wall-eyed and very much on the verge of middle age. She clucked around in her hennish way for a while and then Mickey took the letter out of the table drawer. "I guess this must be what you were looking for," he said. "It'd fallen behind the table."

The day nurse unfolded the letter and folded it again rapidly after a quick glance. Mickey saw a little bloom of pink on her cheeks, as if she had been slapped. He could have kicked himself. He should have torn up the letter and thrown it out of the window rather than put himself through this scene. But maybe she would just take the letter and get the hell out of the room without saying anything.

Oh, no.

"Thank you very much, Mr. Henry," the nurse said.

"Don't mention it," Mickey said, rolling over and turning his face to the wall.

The day nurse hesitated. "Did you read it, Mr. Henry?" she said at last.

Mickey said nothing, vainly pretending to be asleep.

"Did you, Mr. Henry?"

Mickey groaned. "Well, er," he said.

"I can see you did!" said the day nurse triumphantly. "So, having read it, what did you think of it?"

There was a long pause.

"What did you think of it, Mr. Henry?" the day nurse repeated in an even more piercing voice. "Well?"

Oh, God, Mickey groaned. "Why, very pretty, I'm sure," he said feebly.

The day nurse snorted. "Pretty!" she said. "It's perfectly terrible, and you know it very well!"

Mickey could not have been more surprised if she had snatched up the water jug and poured it over his head. He turned over again and sat up, staring at her uncomprehendingly.

"Perfectly terrible!" she repeated, unfolding the letter and glaring at it. "All this sheer—sheer *gook*! *My priceless Rapture!*

37

Twin oases of serene blue! There lives no man who, after but one glance at those treasures, could refrain from yearning to crush them 'neath the fevered impress of his own! Of his own treasures, the hopeless imbecile is saying, only of course he doesn't realize it. Oh, how *revolting*!—but it was the best I could find."

Mickey felt his mouth gaping open like a goldfish's. "The best you could find?"

"I know it's hard to believe," the day nurse said, "but it's true. Apparently there just aren't any books of contemporary love letters being published. Finally in a second-hand bookstore on Fourth Avenue the man brought this out, apologetically, I must say that for him, and said he was sorry but it was the best he could do. Published in 1870-something. The engravings should have warned me, flowers and cupids, you know, but there wasn't anything else, and I was desperate, so I bought it.

"I read all the letters in the book that night at home and really, I thought I was going to be ill; and yet—you see, I'd tried myself, but it wasn't any good, I simply couldn't write a convincing letter. If I'd had any love letters of my *own*, you know, from when I was a girl, but—well, I hadn't. And as I thought this was the least horrible of the lot I copied it."

"You mean you wrote that down out of a *book*?" Mickey said.

"Why, yes, Mr. Henry. That's what I've been trying to tell you."

"But why?"

The nurse sat down. "I'm sorry," she apologized. "That's just like me, starting the wrong way round. It was to cheer someone up, Mr. Henry. You see, I've another patient on this floor—it's a young woman, and the long and short of it is—well," said the nurse, "the long and short of it is, she's never had any love letters either, not if *I* know anything, and I do, out of my own experience, or lack of it, you might say—and if there's anybody I've ever seen who needs more than anything else in the world to get a nice sweet romantic letter from a young man, she does."

"What's the matter with her?" Mickey asked.

"Oh, things," said the nurse.

"What kind of things?"

"Just—complications."

Her tone, suddenly cool and professional, put an end to that line of inquiry. Anyway, Mickey reflected, what did he care? "Well," he said, "if she's in a poor state of health, I'll tell you one thing—you give her that letter and the shock'll kill her." And he lay down again and closed his eyes to indicate that his interest in the subject was ended.

"I'm sorry to have taken so much of your time, Mr. Henry," the nurse said, and left him to his cherished solitude.

Mickey dozed fitfully until the noon hour, when the nurse delivered his lunch. He ate it without pleasure. She came back for the tray and half-emptied dishes, picked them up in silence and started for the door again when Mickey cleared his throat. The nurse glanced at him over her shoulder.

"What's she like?" Mickey said.

"Who, Mr. Henry?"

"Girl with the twin oases."

The nurse put the tray down. "Well," she said, "I could tell you she's very pretty, couldn't I—I mean, very pretty when she's well and has her colour back and isn't as thin as a shadow, poor dear—but that would be deceiving you, Mr. Henry. No, I fear she's never been pretty and never will be, even providing she gets over this operation all right."

"What do you mean, you *could* tell me she's very pretty?" Mickey asked. "Why did you say that?"

"Simply because a young man's more apt to get interested in a pretty girl than a plain one, isn't he, Mr. Henry? Or so," said the nurse, "I've always heard."

"But *you* couldn't think of deceiving me."

"It wouldn't be fair, to her nor to you either. I mean, if you

39

became interested in her, Mr. Henry, it should be entirely without illusions."

"Interested in her!" Mickey said with irritation. "Who says I'm going to become interested in her? What's this all about, anyway?"

"I'm sorry, Mr. Henry," the nurse said, picking up the tray again. "It was just an expression, I'm sure."

There was a silence. She was making for the door when again Mickey cleared his throat.

"Did you give her the letter?"

"The twin oases letter, Mr. Henry? No, of course not. After all, you said the shock would kill her."

Mickey frowned at his bony knees, hunched up together under the sheets.

"So what are you going to do?"

"Why," said the nurse, "I don't know. Perhaps it was a foolish idea after all. Although," she added, "getting a nice romantic letter from an unknown young man would be a thrill for a girl like that, particularly in her present condition."

"Yes?" Mickey said. "But if she did get the letter and then found out it was a fake, how would that be doing her any good?"

"She won't find out, Mr. Henry."

"How do you know?"

"I know."

Mickey was still frowning at his knees when the nurse left. After a while he rolled over and closed his eyes, but his afternoon nap proved even more elusive than the morning one. Finally, with an exclamation of disgust, he abandoned the attempt and sat up. Well, all right, he said to himself, if the only way to get some sleep and get back to normal is to write the letter to the damn girl to put her out of your mind, then you better do it.

Yes? he went on. That sounds simple, but what are you going to tell her about? About the fools and barbarians outside and how lucky we are—she and I—to be sealed up here in our little white cocoons? That'd give her a big kick, wouldn't it? She'd think you were nuts.

No. You'd have to tell her all sorts of stuff—well, about things the way life used to seem to you. I mean, getting up in the morning, and the first good cup of coffee, and the bright fall frost on the trees in Central Park, and the tingly clean smell of the air, and the girls' faces, pink and laughing, and their beautiful eyes; and the feeling that you want to run and jump up and smack your heels together like a colt, just for the kick of being young and alive on a frosty golden-leafed fall morning.

And in love.

Sure, you've got to pretend you're in love, so as to write to her in the proper way. . . .

Mickey scrabbled around in the drawer of the utility table and found a pencil and a piece of paper. With his tongue between his teeth he addressed himself to the painful intellectual struggle of imagining that he was in love with life and with a girl. He found shortly that the struggle was even more difficult when undertaken sitting up in bed. He peered speculatively at the clothes closet. Inside, unseen for weeks, were his dressing-gown and his slippers. Mickey made up his mind to it, swung his legs over the side of the bed, and stood on his feet.

The whole room described a magnificent swoop and plunge, as if the hospital had suddenly turned itself into an ocean liner tossing in a mid-Atlantic gale, and Mickey found himself hanging on to the bed for dear life. Presently the gale abated, the waves turned into silky little billows; the clothes closet straightened itself out and began to seem attainable. Mickey let go of the bed and took a step forward. His knees quivered and he threatened to fall.

"No!" he said in a loud voice. "Not going to."

As if in answer, the clothes closet seemed to advance magically towards him; there he was with his hand on the door knob, and the door was open, and there were dressing-gowns and slippers—and street clothes, suit and shirt and socks and shoes and hat and overcoat, just where they had been put so very long ago. It was a funny smell they had. Not a bad smell, actually. Not like the hospital smell at all, which had come to seem normal. Quite an exciting smell, when you came right down to it—a smell of the world outside, med school, and fall, leaves and wind, smoke and rain.

In dressing-gown and slippers, Mickey sat down at the table and began to write his letter.

According to the nurse, Mickey's letter—which began with the words Dear One, and went on to say how Mickey had caught a glimpse of her, just the barest glimpse, when being brought to his hospital room, and how he had thought about her, and what he had thought—the letter was a success. "It was a regular little poem, Mr. Henry!" said the nurse, most flatteringly. "All that about taking a walk together in Central Park when you're both up and out of here was simply wonderful!"

It was stupid, but Mickey felt quite a glow. He wrote another letter that afternoon.

All in all, he wrote six letters during the week. By then he was walking around the room vigorously. The doctor contemplated the results of his therapy with undisguised satisfaction; surely he had been very wise to put the boy on the no visiting list—look what it had done for him.

"Now perhaps," he suggested, "you'd like to be seeing your family and friends again? Because soon you won't be able to, you know. I mean, not here in the hospital. Just a few more days and we'll be discharging you."

"Fine," Mickey said. He hesitated. He wanted to apologize to the doctor for the way he had been thinking about him and everyone else just a week or so ago, but it would sound—well, it would sound pretty crazy. Therefore all he said was,

42

"Doctor, I want to tell you I'm grateful for everything you've done."

"Not at all, my boy, not at all," said the doctor cheerfully. "I told you, didn't I, I knew how everything was going to come out?"

Then Mickey discovered that the thought of leaving the hospital still gave him a feeling of dismay. Not because he shrank from the world outside; he looked forward to rejoining it; but the thought of never having seen her, the girl he had been writing to, the girl whose response to his letters had, it seemed, done so much for him; for she had flourished, according to the nurse, even as Mickey had. No, he didn't want to identify himself as the letter-writer; but if he could only have a peep at her——

He proposed this to the nurse.

"Certainly," she said, looking up at him and smiling. "I think it will do you good, Mr. Henry."

"What room is she in?"

"414. The door's open. Just have a peep in, as you say."

Mickey adjusted his dressing-gown, opened the door and went down the hall to have a peep at the girl in room 414.

"And I want to tell you," Mickey said, concluding this story, "I was in a sweat. It was a big moment, actually—and sort of sad, too. I mean, she'd got all those letters, and pretty *good* letters, if I do say so, but—well, this was the end. I mean there never was going to be that walk in Central Park I'd talked about. I owed that walk to her, really—if I ever walked there in the future with *any* girl, it would be due to the girl in the hospital room. Writing to her had cleared my mind of all that sick nonsense and made me want to live again. But I wasn't in love with her."

"So what happened?" I burst out as he paused tantalizingly.

"Why don't you go and ask her?" Mickey suggested.

"Go and ask the girl herself?"

43

"The girl herself."

"She won't mind?"

He shook his head.

I took him at his word. Room 414, he had said. I passed Room 409, 410, 411, 412. The next room was a little cubbyhole where the nurses kept their things. A pleasant looking woman in white was sitting there, bent over a sheet of records. "Excuse me," I said, interrupting her work, "but I can't seem to find Room 414."

"Room 414?" she repeated, turning around. "Why, there isn't any."

"There isn't any!" I repeated, amazed. "But Mr. Henry said——"

"Well," amended the nurse, and I noticed that one of her eyes was just a little off centre, and realized that this must be the day nurse that Mickey had told us about, "I suppose you might, if you wanted to, call *this* Room 414."

After a while I realized what she meant. There never had been any Room 414. Room and patient had been invented in the nurse's mind, to save not an imaginary but a real patient's life.

And so I learned that it is retiring from life—as Mickey had —that ages one before one's time.

EAST SIDE HOSPITAL

The Odd Behaviour of Dr. Carl Borger

OFTEN IN YOUR EMBATTLED LIFE AS AN INTERNE YOU FEEL there is no such thing as privacy in the world; the whole vast organization of the hospital seems to be devoted to the proposition that never on any account can you be left alone. If you are lucky enough to discover some neat little hideaway where you fancy you may snatch a few winks, as sure as death and taxes the ceiling will develop a leak, the plumbers will arrive, or the painters, or both, or one of the lady cats that have such a sure scent for hospitals when in the family way. Every hand is against the interne; all men, women, children and cats unite enthusiastically in the great experiment of finding out whether new young doctors can exist without sleep, and for how long.

We were never actually off duty when we were supposed to be through with our labours. Any one of a dozen things might happen, not the least of which would be filling in for a fellow interne on the sick list. Eyes grainy with fatigue, I remember wandering around in a kind of headachy fog. Any number of times I felt quite sure that some horrible disaster was going to strike me or one of the patients I attended.

Certainly I thought the fated occasion had arrived when I was attending a very large and very noisy expectant mother. Upon seeing me she inquired of God and the world at large if they were robbing the kindergarten for doctors these days, and bade me go and fetch a real man. I told her it was too bad, she was stuck with me and I with her and we had to make the best of it. Fortunately everything went forward on schedule, just

45

as it was supposed to according to the book; and between us we managed to produce a fine baby boy. Her opinion of me somewhat improved, the new mother handed out a grudging smile and then asked me what I was waiting for.

"The after-birth," I informed her.

At this a new expression crossed her face, one of alarm.

"Nothing to be concerned about," I assured her. "It's the regular thing."

Her face twisted even more grotesquely.

"For goodness' sake," I said, "what's the trouble?"

She let out a yell. "The pain, Doctor, the pain!"

"The pain?" I said. "Where?"

She pointed vaguely to her stomach. "Oh my God," she cried, "it's killing me!"

This, of course, was nonsense; no pain was to be expected; it had absolutely no business being there. "You must be mistaken," I said nervously.

All her previous doubts of my competence were confirmed. "Young dummy!" she shouted. "You think I don't know a pain when I got it?" And she clutched at herself as if in agony.

Nothing I knew, nothing I had been taught, nothing within the experience of the whole medical profession seemed to me to offer a reasonable answer to the mystery of why a woman should experience something apparently approximating the pains of childbirth *after* having given birth.

A series of shattering screams rang in the air. "Do something!" she bawled; but what could I do? Then as I stared and sweated, the mystery began to dissolve. She hadn't overstated the case when she called me a young dummy. There was good reason for these new, inexplicable pains.

Twins.

The second boy came along handily too. Later on, with her infant sons nestled beside her, my patient forgave me for my sins. "Doctor," she said generously. "I'm telling you what I'm going to do; I'm going to publish you all over!"

In those days the interne received a dollar a day, snatched his meals when he could, and got one day off every two or three weeks. He shared sleeping quarters in the hospital with three brother internes. His most hated assignment was in emergency receiving during the long bitter hours from midnight to dawn. These are the hours of the witches' sabbath, when the most ridiculous, most impossible, most gruesome accidents and slaughterings and love battles and brawls take place; when the drunks cavort and plunge headlong into trucks, cars and taxis and glass windows and cellars and manholes and topple down subway stairs. Our task was to assess the damage, patch up the victims, commit them to a ward if the injury was serious, release them if it was only superficial.

That seems sensible enough; in reality, there was often no rhyme or reason to what went on; you found yourself in a nightmare world, which perhaps in the next second or two would become merely sheerly ludicrous, subduing the topers' fits, keeping an eye open for their sudden retchings. It was amazing what they could live through; ears, noses, hands sliced off by shattered glass, they would still blearily insist there was nothing wrong, eye you hopefully through the bloody snarl of their face, and request a nickel for a cup of coffee.

But there were pleasanter sides to the treadmill. There was, for instance, W. Hugo Foote—charming, gentle, fantastic W. Hugo, who turned up during clinic hours for certain delicate and exceedingly painful medications, which W. Hugo took uncomplainingly, like the gallant old gentleman he was.

I met W. Hugo first not in the clinic but outside the hospital one afternoon when my fellow interne Sammy Lee and I were getting a breath of air. Slowly proceeding down First Avenue, there came a plump white-bearded rosy-faced individual clad in frock coat and striped trousers and wheeling a baby carriage in front of him.

"Hello there, Hugo," Sammy called out; and the old gent paused and nodded.

"Good morning, sir," he replied formally. "You find your-self well, I trust?"

"Tip-top. Meet my friend Max," said Sammy affably.

The old boy bowed low. "Honoured, sir," he declared, and reaching into a waistcoat pocket, pulled out a card which he gravely handed to me. On it was printed:

W. HUGO FOOTE
oddments

His mild, beaming smile, his spotless white beard and soup-strainer moustache and the pinkish dome of his bald head were irresistibly reminiscent of the White Knight. And certainly that benign warrior's warsteed, with the beehive and the carrots and the stepladder, bore a close family resemblance to Mr. Foote's baby carriage. Though definitely a baby carriage, it was babyless; instead of an infant it contained a remarkable collection of junk—though the word junk is a disparaging one; I should say instead, *oddments*. I dimly recognized the entrails of an ancient clothes wringer, the florid countenance of a grandfather clock long since silent, an uneasy mass of bed-springs, a covey of vases of different sizes and conditions of ill health, a few discouraged-looking mops, a broom rapidly ap-proaching complete baldness—and, yes, the final glorious White Knight touch, even a mouse trap.

These oddments, I learned, W. Hugo Foote collected in daily scavenging trips all over the East Side. He sold them for what they would bring to the junk shops on East Third and Fourth Streets. Occasionally there would be a windfall: by mis-chance, oversight or accident some object of genuine value would find its way into the refuse cans that constituted W. Hugo's field of operations. Then for a few days or a week or two—depending on how much the prize had brought—the East Side would know Mr. Foote no more.

Stabling the baby carriage, brushing his top hat to a rich

sheen, taking out his ivory handled walking stick, he would saunter up Fifth Avenue, register at a good hotel, and generally behave like a retired millionaire resting on his laurels. Money spent, he would fade gently from the scene, and out would come the baby carriage once more.

But whichever phase he was in, the collector of oddments or the millionaire, W. Hugo's uniform—frock coat and striped trousers—remained the same. It was interesting to devise reasons for this eccentricity, and we speculated that he had fallen from high estate through the machinations of unscrupulous enemies but still insisted on wearing the clothes he had been accustomed to as fortune's favourite.

The truth, alas, was quite another story; but now that I consider it, perhaps in its way more interesting. W. Hugo Foote had begun his commercial career as a clerk in one of the great department stores. Through diligent work and the increasing distinction of his appearance, he had soared high—to the position, no less, of chief floorwalker. Year after year he had patrolled the store aisles, magnificent in frock coat and striped trousers, fresh carnation in buttonhole every day, linen immaculate, shoes burnished to a glow; a kingly male indeed, soothing the breasts of ferocious women shoppers, ladling out advice and encouragement to all who applied. And so he might have continued, full of honours and glory, to the end of his days and been put out to pasture in the mellow evening sunlight, had it not been for an unfortunate discovery.

It seemed that there was one tiny crack in the stately façade of W. Hugo Foote. A trifling weakness, true, but still a weakness, particularly to be regretted in the person of a floorwalker. Mr. Foote himself freely admitted this. It had grown on him, he confessed after having been caught in the very act—grown on him, Mr. Foote confessed, in spite of his most strenuous battles to oppose it.

In short, he had been altogether unable to resist the temptation to pick up little bits and pieces, odds and ends, from the store counters as he strolled solemnly past and tuck them up his sleeves and into his pockets.

He didn't sell any of this loot, he simply added it to the hoard in his furnished room; and occasionally he would finger through the pile and wonder what on earth had compelled him to pilfer this magpie treasure: thimbles, cuff links, scissors, measuring tape, ashtrays, paper-weights, needles and pins and paperclips.

The store did not prosecute, merely fired him; but Mr. Foote knew he could never return to similar employment. The fact was, the disease was incurable, the craving was still in him, he had to satisfy it. He found a way.

So now W. Hugo Foote patrolled the aisles of an infinitely greater department store, the streets and alleys and byways of the East Side, pausing to pluck desirable items here and there and tuck them into the baby carriage—still splendid in frock coat and striped trousers, a happy man.

In contrast, there was Dr. Carl Borger.

W. Hugo Foote lived on a few dollars a month (excepting the periods of great prosperity); Carl Borger on a few thousand. Dr. Borger was by long odds the most brilliant surgeon attached to the hospital staff at that time. We all admired him and despised him. I think I hated him more even than the others did, for reasons that will become evident.

A man of medium height, inclined to fleshiness, with broad shoulders, stringy brown hair and a seedy moustache set in a pouchy, pasty face, Dr. Borger's taste in clothes was what even we poverty-stricken internes recognized as appalling. He favoured perfectly dreadful shirts, silk, striped in green or lavender or pink, above which he wore a high, choking kind of collar. His suits were noisy too. A final touch must be added. Dr. Borger was seldom seen without a woozy cigar butt drooping from his lips, a vile relic that seemed to have been soaking there for days.

Out of his operating gown, no one would have suspected the genius that lay in those pudgy fingers and behind the pale forehead, though to be sure Dr. Borger's eyes hinted at the presence within him of a great surgeon: swift, penetrating, lively eyes. Occasionally, had we thought to look deep enough, we might have found in those eyes the feverish glow of a man driven almost to the point of desperation. But none of us did.

This fattish, vulgar-looking man owned a boiling temper and a tongue like a scalpel. He could make you sizzle helplessly all day. He had perceived that I was in love (as we were all in love) with beautiful Jenny Aldredge, our darling student nurse. Others were able to chat airily and dashingly with Jenny; I never could; I was too shy. Not for all the world would I have admitted the tender sentiments that engulfed me as I gazed at Jenny; my face was rigidly disciplined, my eyes cold, while within I quivered, sighed, mooed with love. And the devilish Borger saw this state of affairs and shot his stiletto home.

"Ah, Jenny, my dear," he said one day in his hateful, sneering voice, "don't you get tired once in a while of carrying all those disgusting pots and pans around? I'll give you a tip. Let our young doctor here"—he waved his cigar butt in my direction—"give you a hand. He'd be delighted to. You see, Jenny, the young doctor worships at your shrine. Look at him blush, Jenny! Just look!" And with a chuckle the brute strode off, while I practically ran in the other direction.

This was bad enough; what followed was worse. It happened when I was assisting Dr. Borger at an operation. Despise and try to avoid him as we did, all was different when it came to the operating room; you counted it a privilege to assist him, for from no one else could you learn so much. The mean, irascible, vulgar Carl Borger was gone; here instead was the man of magic, the genius, the god. The sureness of his technique was incredible, and his searching mind was always yards ahead of yours, probing through the problems to be faced like a beam of light, scrutinizing and solving, and making the whole thing seem as simple as adding up two and two.

It was very hot that day; the operation was a long one; the sweat streamed off us. Borger thought I was slow in applying an artery clamp, as I am sure I must have been; no one could match or come anywhere near his blinding speed. Swiftly he snatched up another clamp. "Stupid!" he grunted, and rapped me across the knuckles.

That may not sound like much—the baton giving a whack of reproof, the schoolteacher's ruler. Believe me, it was a mortal insult. I could have hit him. Hit him? Cut his throat, rather, the swine, the lout! Somehow or other I'd get back at Carl Borger.

We went ahead with the operation; somehow I managed to finish up without a mistake, though I saw Borger through a haze of fury. In the doctors' dressing-room later we washed and dressed. Borger didn't glance at me, said nothing. He dressed in a great hurry and made off like a man with an urgent errand on his mind.

Leaving the dressing-room, I saw that he had gone to a pay telephone booth down the corridor. Through the glass doors I could see him talking earnestly. Impossible, of course, to hear what he was saying. It occurred to me now that I had seen him behave in exactly the same way many times before—dash out of the dressing room and down to this booth. But why? Why, when there was a private telephone for the doctors' own use in the dressing-room? Why should he prefer the hot, smelly booth?

The answer to that was easy. You prefer a booth to a phone out in the open when you don't want anyone to hear what you're saying.

And why shouldn't he want anyone to hear what he was saying? Because it must be embarrassing to him. Something he was ashamed of.

I felt inestimably better. Dr. Borger, I told myself, I am

going to find out just what goes on in that telephone booth—
an illicit romance—a love nest—your shameful secret, whatever it is—and I shall tip off one of the scandal sheets and the
next thing you know you'll be immortalized by some delightful headline such as "Eminent Medico Spurns Blonde Sweetie,"
and that, Dr. Borger, will be the end of you.

In short, Dr. Borger, as my mother of twins said, I am going
to publish you all over!

This was all very well; but I did not pause to reflect how I
proposed to get myself into the telephone booth with Dr.
Borger so unobtrusively that although he would have his
elbows jammed into my stomach or my knee into his he would
fail to notice my presence: because how can you hear what a
man is saying in a glass-enclosed booth unless you get into it
along with him?

In any event, I never had to solve the problem. My whole
scheme of revenge blew up.

Borger was in the phone booth again and again and I would
do my best to be lurking somewhere in the neighbourhood,
hoping that he would forget to close the glass door and let me
overhear what he was saying. When he came out of the booth,
he looked terrible; God knows he never was prepossessing in
appearance but now he resembled a tragic clown. He caught
sight of me and his pasty face flushed.

"Is this all you've got to do, bum around in the hallways?"
he shouted, and stalked off, muttering gibberish.

If looks could kill, he would have dropped dead.

I stepped out into one of the areaways to cool off and found
someone else there, also cooling off. It was Sammy Lee, my
friend and colleague, moodily pulling on a cigarette. "That
bastard Borger," he burst out, seeing me. "You know what
he told me just now, for no damn reason at all? 'Lee,' he said,
'you think you're going to be a surgeon, do you? Take my
advice and get into something you can handle, street-cleaning
or some similar line, before it's too late.' Just meanness,"

Sammy said, "just pure downright damnable meanness. The kind of thing you'll brood over, and he knows it."

"Listen to *me*," I said, and told him about the humiliating Jenny Aldredge incident, and the rap across the knuckles, and a dozen other slights and slurs.

"If you ask me," Sammy said, "the guy's going nuts."

"He was born that way," I said. "Loud-mouthed, dumb, stupid, vulgar, ignorant, prejudiced, cockeyed, mean little inferior-minded sadist. He was born that way and also, I agree with you, also he is going out of his mind. Something is working on him, some secret. I don't know what it is, but I'm going to find out. He's got a glare in his eyes like a madman. One of these days he's going to fall over in a fit, frothing at the mouth, and they'll have to slap him into a straitjacket and haul him off kicking and screaming."

"Just grant me one thing, merciful Father and Saviour," said Sammy piously, "let me be the guy who slaps him into the straitjacket."

"This here is Dr. Carl Borger you are talking about?" someone said.

Sammy and I looked around. A small faded-looking man in dingy clothes had come up behind us. He had a creased greyish face and nervous fingers that squirmed and clung together, and his dark eyes had an expression of shock.

"Dr. *Carl* Borger?" he said again.

"You bet you," Sammy said. "The prize medical rump in this whole outfit."

"And he is all you say?"

"More," Sammy said forcefully. "Much, much more."

"Holy Mother!" cried the small grey man. "What can I do?"

"What's your trouble, friend?" Sammy asked.

"This Dr. Borger, this madman, he's the man who is going to operate on my little kid to-morrow!"

There was a great silence. Sammy and I looked at each

other. Then Sammy threw down his cigarette and deliberately ground it under with his heel. "Now listen," he said, "just take it easy and listen. Ever since I was a kid, thirteen or fourteen, I aimed at being a doctor, a surgeon. It hasn't been easy, it's a kind of tough grind, but I've had one lucky break. One big lucky break. That's having a guy like Carl Borger to show me just what being a real *good* surgeon, just about the best in the world, really means."

"That goes for me too," I said.

"But," objected the newcomer, "you said——"

"That was sour grapes," I said.

"Sour grapes?"

"I mean," I said, "a great doctor like Dr. Borger, who knows just about everything there is to know about the human body and how to operate on it, naturally he gets a little impatient once in a while with young doctors like Dr. Lee here and me who pull some pretty dumb stunts sometimes, and so he—well, you understand, he bawls us out, says things he doesn't actually mean. Well, we know that, but still, we've got to blow off steam, try to kid ourselves we never do anything wrong, it's all his fault; so, you see——"

"You see," said Sammy, "that's why you heard us saying all that crap."

"Crap?"

"Bolony," said Sammy. "Just pure junk. I want to tell you the honest-to-God truth: you ought to go down on your knees and give thanks you've got Dr. Borger to operate on your kid."

The small man's face was looking reasonably human again. "You mean all this?" he said.

"Please," Sammy said gently, putting his hand on the other's arm, "please, believe us."

He searched our faces; then he smiled and nodded. "I do," he said. "Thank you."

When he was gone, Sammy took out a cigarette and had a long pull. "Gee," he said simply.

"But it's true, you know," I said.

"Sure I know it's true," Sammy said. "He's still a heel, all the same."

"Absolutely," I said. "A grade-A louse."

The operation the next morning was a success, and the patient—a twelve-year-old girl—did not die; for that she had the skill of Dr. Borger's hands to thank. Afterward, Borger did not bolt off down the hall to the telephone booth but remained in the dressing-room.

"Do you mind waiting a few minutes?" he said to me when I started to leave. "I'd like to have a few words with you."

What had I done now, I wondered. "Of course not, sir," I said.

"And with Dr. Lee."

"Dr. Lee?"

"I asked him to stop in here too."

A moment or two later Sammy came into the room. His expression showed that he was as mystified as I.

"Gentlemen," Carl Borger said, "I have an apology to make to both of you. More than one apology; a dozen apologies. There's no excuse for my conduct but at least there is a reason behind it, which I should like to tell you about."

He took out one of his horrible cigars, bit into it nervously but did not light it.

"These last few weeks I've been in a terrible mess," he resumed. "A friend gave me a tip on what he said was a sure thing in the stock market. It turned out to be nothing of the sort but I was too deeply in to get out. All I could think of was those damned figures, figures, figures, the latest quotation. I couldn't confide in anyone, I was ashamed of what I'd done, the sucker I'd turned out to be. I hated that phone booth outside in the hall like an instrument of torture, yet I couldn't keep away from it, for that was where I'd call my broker and learn the latest bad news.

"Yesterday was the worst—not only the worst, it was the end. I hung up and then sat there staring at my fingers. That was all I had left now, those ten fingers. There seemed to be some awful curse on me, for as I stared at them I thought I saw them change and grow wrinkled and arthritic and useless. I rubbed them together in a panic to destroy the illusion but there was no feeling in them. I was a pauper and as a surgeon I was finished.

"Well, it was a pretty bad moment. I left the booth and saw you"—he nodded to me—"and burst out at you with something or other, I don't know what. In fact for the next hour I don't know what I did. Then I realized that someone was speaking to me, someone that so far as I knew I'd never seen before. 'Dr. Borger?' he was saying. 'You're Dr. Borger?' 'Yes,' I said, 'I'm Dr. Borger'—the ex-Dr. Borger, I might have said, 'What about it?' 'Dr. Borger,' he said, 'I just wanted to tell you I know I'm lucky to have you as doctor for my kid.' 'What makes you think so?' I said. 'Why,' he said, 'those young fellows, young doctors who work with you. I just been talking with them. You know what they think of you, Dr. Borger? Why, they say you are the greatest man in the world!'

"I stared at him. 'Who says this?' I said incredulously. He described both of you, and I recognized you from his description. And you'd said that about me, when God knows how miserably I'd been treating you. I felt—I can't tell you how I felt. All I can say is, Thank you, and apologize."

Carl Borger held up his ten fingers and smiled at them and at us.

"I guess there's still some life left in them," he said. "Anyway, you boys think so, don't you?" He fumbled in his pocket. "Here," he concluded, "have a cigar, please!"

It was extraordinary how the atmosphere changed after this incident. Of course there was still too much work, and we never managed to get enough sleep, and people went right on having crises and producing babies at the most inconvenient hours—but Sammy and I no longer seemed to mind so much. As Mr. W. Hugo Foote observed one day in the out-patient clinic, where we were taking care of him on one of his regular visits: "Gentlemen, I don't know if you're aware of it, but there's been a big improvement in both of you lately. If you will not consider it presumptuous of me, I'd be inclined to remark that you've hit on a secret I found out for myself some time ago—how to adjust yourselves to your work. Believe me, it's the greatest thing in life for keeping young and keeping happy!"

The real reason, of course, was that our master, our god, was no longer an enemy but a friend. Such was the effect of those few words on the irascible Carl Borger. Never, Sammy and I resolved, had there been a happier accident than that the little grey man should have overheard us that day. Not only did it bring about a change in Dr. Borger but also, through him, in us too.

The Man Who Grew Young Overnight

THOUGH AT TIMES IT SEEMS TO YOU THAT YOU ARE FATED TO remain an interne for ever, the end comes at last and you are free to go whither you will, depending on your taste, ambition and the amount of money in your pocket. I had little of the latter but enough—through my family's kindness—to manage a year's study of plastic surgery in Europe. Then I rented an office in New York and sat down to wait for patients.

I say "sat down to wait for patients." How easily one writes the phrase, how many young doctors have said it or written it before, and how untrue it is! You don't sit and wait, you try to keep busy. I cleaned house and made and drank a lot of coffee and wondered who my first patient would be. Actually my very first patient was more or less dragged to the office by a friend; but I dreamed of more distinguished fare, *and* a patient who would come absolutely under his own power, let us say a tall aristocrat from Old Westbury, bluest of blue bloods, with tanned cheeks, smart Guards moustache, beautifully tailored tweeds.

And a perfectly horrible nose.

I invented a whole history for that nose. This nose had been sniffing the air of the field of battle—the polo field—when the swing of an enemy mallet had caught it flush on its bridge, creating a situation that caused its owner to shudder inside his camel's hair coat whenever he caught sight of the ghastly thing in a mirror. But despair not; be of good heart—Maltz is available. Ah, how available he is, how extremely available!

59

"Rest easy, sir," I would say in dulcet tones to the ravaged polo player. "Soon we shall rehabilitate your nose; nay, we shall do more—we shall make it more distinguished than ever. Kindly step this way."

So cosy and intimate had I become with the vision of this rich, aristocratic nose that when the doorbell rang one sunny morning the conviction transfixed my mind that this was he, the polo player. I flung aside the cleaning rag, adjusted my smile and the furniture, put on the freshly ironed white coat, bustled to the front door and looked up expectantly.

In that at least my vision did not fail me—it was necessary to look up. My caller towered overhead; he was a fraction over six feet four. In no other respect did he bear the slightest resemblance to my dream-world Old Westburian. True, the suit he wore was quite decent, his Panama hat eminently respectable, his shoes tidy, his shirt clean; but there was nothing wrong with his nose, and his complexion was a mild shade of cocoa.

"Are you Dr. Maltz?" the giant asked in a very deep voice.

"I am," I said. "What can I do for you?"

"Sir," he said, "I want you to give me a white man's lip."

His underlip, I saw, protruded a good deal, but so do the underlips of many people who own the kind of skin we call white.

"How did you happen to hear of me, Mr.——?"

"My name, sir," said the giant, with the same deep melancholy, "is Russell. A friend of mine works in the neighbourhood where your mother lives, and your mother was talking about you—as mothers will, sir, as mothers will—and my friend chanced to hear what she said, and told me. I had not known there were doctors who do your kind of work. I resolved then and there to come and ask you to give me a white man's lip."

"Where did you get this idea of 'a white man's lip,' Mr. Russell?" I asked. "There's nothing wrong with your lip. It's somewhat pendulous but not enough to be noticeable on a man of your height."

"It is not my idea, sir, it is hers," Mr. Russell replied. And then, without the least trace of embarrassment, he continued simply: "You see, sir, I am in love. She is an extremely beautiful woman and extremely proud and she has notified me that she is ashamed to be seen on the public thoroughfares or in public gathering places in my company because of the formation of my lip."

It was impossible not to like Mr. Russell. He had great dignity and great melancholy and the rhythm of his speech had a courtly old-world air; he seemed at once to come from an old, a very old culture and to be absurdly young—a great tall man, sweet, simple, and full of sorrows.

"I don't want to offend you, Mr. Russell," I said, "but do you think a woman who behaves like that can really be very much in love with you?"

"You do not offend me, sir," Mr. Russell said with a wonderful slow smile. "No; as I remarked, the question is one of pride. She fancies my lip is a hurt to her pride." He reflected on this for a moment or two and then, taking off the Panama hat and gazing at it absently, he added: "But it avails nothing, sir. The fact of the matter is, I am in her spell, and obliged to do all she asks."

"Mr. Russell," I said, "it is quite true that these things can be done, but unfortunately they are very expensive."

"How expensive, sir?"

"To give you a new lip would cost you twelve hundred dollars."

His huge, sad face wrinkled slowly.

"Twelve hundred dollars, sir?"

"Twelve hundred dollars."

The announcement had the desired effect.

"I am afraid, sir, that is beyond my means."

"I'm sorry, Mr. Russell."

He replaced the Panama and bowed to me. "You have been kind, sir, to give me your attention. I wish you good morning."

I thought that would be the last of Mr. Russell, and I thought I had acted for the best. I composed myself to more waiting. But it was not for long. The next morning the doorbell rang again.

There he was. He had a small black valise in his hand.

"May I come in, sir?"

With immense solemnity he advanced into the waiting-room. Opening the black bag he turned it upside down over the table. A stream of bills poured out, old, ragged bills, so worn and creased they looked like the tired limp leaves that fall at the end of summer.

"There are twelve hundred one-dollar bills there, sir," said Mr. Russell. "We shall count them, shall we?"

I couldn't believe my eyes.

"Where did you get all this?"

"By saving, sir."

"By saving? Are you sure?"

He gazed at me with wounded eyes. "Of course I am sure, sir. How else would I obtain the money?"

I begged his pardon humbly. "You see, Mr. Russell, I confess I didn't think you'd be able to get so much together. So it was something of a shock."

"If you didn't think I'd be able to assemble the amount you requested, sir, why did you ask for it?"

"I wanted you to give up the idea of having the operation."

Mr. Russell rubbed his face for a moment or two, then drew a breath so deep that his great chest swelled. I thought he was about to lose his temper, but not at all; the deep voice was gentle and sad as ever. "Sir," he said, "when first I came to see you yesterday, I was under the conviction that you were the only doctor of your kind. It now occurs to me that where

there is one there must be others, as it is with everything else
in the world. Is that right, sir?"

"Quite right."

"Then, sir, if you refuse to change my lip for me, I shall
search and I shall search until I find a doctor of your kind who
will."

I believed him. It was hard, though, to believe that any
woman, no matter how beautiful, how proud, would reject
this tall, soft-spoken, decent man because his underlip was a
trifle too large for her taste. I thought it a good deal more
likely that she was merely amusing herself by putting him
through the hoops, posing him one task after another, cruel,
humiliating and needless, to prove her power over the sad,
amiable giant.

"Mr. Russell," I said, "did you tell your friend how much
the operation would cost?"

"Are you asking, sir, about the woman I love?"

"Yes."

"I did not, sir. She said to me, 'If you want me'—a sweet
voice she has, sir, as sweet as violins—'if you want me,' she
said, 'you must arrange to have another lip made, for that lip
I cannot tolerate, Mr. Russell. And until you do,' she said, 'I
wish to see you no more. I refuse to see you.'"

"So you've said nothing to her since then?"

"Nothing, sir."

"Mr. Russell," I said, "I've changed my mind. I'm going
to operate on your lip."

He grasped my shoulders in his enormous hands.

"You're a *good* man, sir!"

"But not for twelve hundred dollars."

"Ah, sir," he declared mournfully, "that is not fair of you,
no, it is not at all fair. That is all the savings I have in the
world, and yet you ask me to try to find additional dollars."

"I don't mean I'm going to charge you *more*, I mean I'm
going to charge you *less*. However, only on one condition.

63

You must promise me that when you see your friend again, after the operation, you will tell her that it *did* cost you twelve hundred dollars."

We made that bargain.

It is no very great matter to decrease the size of a protuberant lip. The operation is performed under local anæsthesia. You cut the excess tissue from inside the lip, approximate the edges of the wound with very fine silk, and bandage the lip outside to support it. Everything is over within half an hour. The patient returns two or three times to be treated and have the bandages changed; a week later the last one is removed. Since all the surgical work is done inside the lip, there is no exterior scar.

So it was with Mr. Russell. The operation was performed that same day; God knows I had no appointments to interfere with it. He came back twice during the following week, and seven or eight days later I took off the last bandage and showed him his new lip. He turned from side to side in front of the three-way mirror, smiling carefully.

"It won't break," I assured him. "It's yours for good."

"I'm sure she will have no complaint now," Mr. Russell said, and there was no sadness left in his voice. The mirror image grinned like a small boy. "It is precisely what she asked me to do for her!"

"Are you going to see her to-day?"

"At six p.m., sir."

"Will you call me afterwards to let me know what she thinks of it?"

He was pleased. "You are sincerely interested, sir?"

"I am indeed."

"I shall be happy to call. But of course"—Mr. Russell touched the new lip tenderly—"I know what she will have to say. She will give it her unreserved approval."

He got up to go, and buried my hand in his.

"You'll remember our agreement, won't you, Mr. Russell?"

"You refer to the fee you are supposed to have charged me, sir?"

"Twelve hundred dollars."

"Yes, sir," Mr. Russell said happily. "I shall inform her that your fee for the operation was twelve hundred dollars."

I watched him through the window as he strode away, head high in the sunlight. He was such a commanding, joyous sight that many people turned round to look at him.

I left the office at about seven that evening; Mr. Russell had yet to call. That was true the next day too, and the next evening. It was true all week. I wasn't surprised; I thought he would still be in a state of shock. It would take him several days to get over the discovery that his lady did not give a damn if he had a big lip or a small lip but that she cared very power-fully that he had thrown away twelve hundred dollars—as Mr. Russell had promised to tell her. When I saw or heard from him next I felt confident that he would be in the condi-tion known as sadder but wiser. In this I was correct, or perhaps I should say one-half correct.

Several weeks went by. My practice was beginning to show dim, very dim, flutterings of life; I had become bold enough to engage for two hours per day an august, military female who sat at the desk in the waiting-room and impressed callers, or so I hoped. She did, at any rate, impress me. I had just about forgotten Mr. Russell, whereas he should have been on my conscience night and day; for I had stirred up his private life and the consequences might have been explosive.

They were explosive.

The door of the inner office opened and my military lady came in at her sergeant-major step.

"There's a man outside I don't like the looks of, Doctor."

"Yes?" I said.

"A coloured individual."

I put down the photograph I had been examining. Mr. Russell, I thought, Mr. Russell; and my sleeping conscience woke up and gave a nasty twinge. "I'll see him," I said, and went past her into the waiting-room.

It was Mr. Russell, all right, but for a few minutes I didn't think so. The Panama hat was approximately the same, but nothing else was. The stalwart body had shrunk into itself; there was the tremble of age in his hands—the hand that only a few weeks ago had crushed mine in its great grip now looked feather light. The organ notes of his voice had become shrill and desperate.

"Ah, thank mercy you're here!" he cried. "You must help me, sir, you must!"

"My God, what's happened to you?" I asked.

"It's the bug, sir—the bug!"

The sergeant-major was frowning at us with intense distaste. I pulled Mr. Russell after me into the inside office and shut the door on her superior glare.

"Sit down," I said. "What bug?"

"The African bug, sir," said Mr. Russell, with a sound like a whimper. "It's got me and it won't let me go. It's killing me, sir."

I sat down opposite him. "Tell me everything from the beginning," I said. "You were going to call me, do you remember? Why didn't you?"

"I couldn't, sir. I couldn't find the spirit to call you, though I had promised." Mr. Russell licked his lip, that proud new lip that looked withered too, and his shoulders bowed lower. "The spirit was all thrashed out of me, sir. That was because, you see, I had lived up to my undertaking with you. 'Why, man,' she said, when we met, 'your lip is all changed! 'So it is,' I told her. 'It was your wish, and so it was done.' 'And who did this?' she asked, and I told her. 'And how much did it cost you?' she asked, and I told her. Yes, I told her. 'Twelve hundred dollars,' I said."

Mr. Russell put his hands over his face and moaned a little to himself.

"Sir, sir, I thought she would—I thought some grievous thing would happen. I am not exaggerating, sir, I have never seen a woman look so. A beautiful woman, sir, as I have told you, as beautiful as the summer morn. But when I spoke the words 'twelve hundred dollars,' a change such as I have never seen came over her. It was another woman sitting there, and this woman was as horrible to see as a witch. 'You had twelve hundred dollars,' this witch woman said in a little far-away voice, 'and you spent it on your lip?' 'I did,' I said. 'It was what you told me should be done, because you were ashamed of me.' 'Twelve hundred dollars,' she said again, 'and you spent it on your lip.'

"She put her head on the table—we were sitting at a table, sir, having tea—and I thought she was crying; so I put my hand on her arm to comfort her. Sir, it was like touching a tiger. Her head sprang up and I swear there was foam on her lips. I cannot repeat the words she spoke then, they are too foul.

"She told me that I was only a—I was only a simple fool, she had never thought me anything but a fool. She had asked me to have my lip changed only because it seemed to her a joke for all the trouble and worry it would give me. She said she had never loved me and never could love me and now that I had spent twelve hundred dollars which should have been hers, I had cheated and deceived her, I had robbed her, and so she was cursing me. She rose from the table and in words that made me shudder she cursed me; and from this curse, she promised me, I would die."

His sunken eyes gazed at me despairingly.

"Oh, the curse, sir, I paid not too much attention to it then. As I said, the spirit was thrashed out of me by my new knowledge. Not only that she had always thought me a fool, sir. What was far worse was the thought that every night of every day I had toadied to her and cosseted after her and begged her to permit me to touch my lips to hers, each of those nights, sir, unbeknownst to me, she had lain in the arms of her true love. For so she told me.

"I went to my room at last. I had no desire for food or drink. I lay in my room thinking of her in another man's arms and I sobbed because it hurt me so much. I lay in my room for four days and in that time I did no more than sip some water, for the thought of food disgusted me. It was on the evening of the fourth day that I remembered the curse."

I interrupted him. "Do you believe in such things?"

"You see me as I sit before you," he said mournfully. "Surely that is the proof that one must believe. And yet before this misery I would have laughed at the notion. I count myself an intelligent man, sir. I had good schooling in Jamaica, where I was born; and my parents were educated people too. Curses and such mumbo jumbo were only for ignorant fellows. Yet —yet—hadn't that woman set spell on me the moment I was introduced to her? Beautiful though she was, as I have told you so often, still was it not extraordinary that it should be but the work of a second for her eyes and her lips and her lovely shape to captivate me entirely? And if she could throw such a spell on me when she had no reason to hate me, though thinking me only a fool, then, when my actions had thrown her into such a convulsion of rage as to bring the foam to her mouth, why, then there must be truth in the curse she had pronounced that I must die! It seemed very reasonable to me, sir. It seemed very reasonable. And look at me for proof!

"My mouth was dry, sir, as I lay there in my room," he continued, "and I would wet it with a few drops of water and run my tongue around inside it. Thus I came to discover the dreadful thing. My landlady, good soul that she was, had become concerned and had endeavoured to tempt my appetite with dainties she herself prepared; but I had no stomach for food, as I have told you. And now my landlady brought a visitor for me. A tiny little fellow he was, but agile, exceedingly agile. He never rested, even as he was examining me, his little head bobbing and swaying and his little feet performing a tattoo—in other circumstances, sir, he would have made me laugh.

"He said to me: 'Have you been in any trouble, son? Any trouble that comes to your mind with anyone?'

" 'You tell him now, Mr. Russell!' my landlady said. 'Dr. Smith here is a true and a good man, and he can help you, if you tell him all!'

" 'Yes, son,' Dr. Smith said, 'you must tell me all, or I am powerless.'

"Therefore I told him about Nina. That is her name, sir, Nina.

"The story appeared to excite him greatly. 'As I thought!' he said in his squeaky monkey voice. 'And now then, tell me this. Has there been any change in your body that you have noticed? Has something appeared on your physique that has not been there before?'

"There was only one thing I could think of. I told him what I had found with my tongue inside my mouth. 'Let me see that!' he cried. 'You let me see that right now!'

"I opened my mouth wide. The good soul my landlady, I remember precisely how she looked, so frightened that it appeared she wished to leave the room but unable to make herself do so because of her anxiety to see what was inside my mouth. Then Dr. Smith lowered his head very close to mine where it lay on the pillow of the bed, and squinting thusly peered into my mouth and at the precise spot I indicated.

"For some seconds he peered in this manner, then his head jerked back in apparent alarm, then came slowly forward again, weaving somewhat from side to side, so that you might have said he was approaching a dangerous animal in the most wary fashion, attempting to seize it by surprise. Even more slowly, with the utmost caution, he raised the forefinger of his right hand and very delicately, sir, very, very delicately he put the tip of it into my mouth. With this tip of his finger he touched the spot I indicated, but for no more, sir, than an instant.

"That instant might have turned his finger into a red-hot poker for all the alarm and shock he now displayed; because he snatched his finger back, sir, and staring at it as if it were in flames and as if the anguish from its fire coursed through his body, he held it high before us and he cried out at the top of his shrill little monkey voice: 'You see that *slime*? You see that evil slime? That is what is killing you—the stinking, festering slime produced by the African bug that is lodged inside your mouth because of the curse that was laid on you!' "

Breathing heavily, again Mr. Russell put his hands over his face, and rubbed them wearily back and forth.

"This thing is really in your mouth?" I said.

"It is there all the time, sir," he said in a mumbling voice from behind his hands. "The little man, this Dr. Smith, or so he is called, declared that he could drive it away, if I would have patience and do as he directed. And indeed I did. I swallowed the liquids he brought me, powerful medicines they were, or so Dr. Smith said, and I rubbed his pastes and his lotions into my mouth, faithfully and with patience, three times a day and once during the night; but all to no avail. Nina's curse was a very powerful curse, Dr. Smith said, it was opposing us with a terrible struggle; but he said I must not despair, for eventually his medicines would prove even more powerful. But, sir"—and he lowered his hands from his shrunken, tragic face—"I felt I could not last. I could feel that —slime, as he called it, infesting my whole body. The dreadful thing burned inside my lip——"

"Your lip?" I said, interrupting him.

Mr. Russell nodded. "I told you, sir, inside my mouth."

"You didn't say on your *lip* before. May I see it?"

He opened his mouth. I pulled out his underlip and touched a spot in the centre.

"Is that it?"

Again he nodded.

"Do you want me to get rid of it?"

"Can you, sir?"

I filled a syringe with novocaine, disinfected his lip and chose a fine knife and forceps from the sterilizer. After the novocaine had taken effect, I removed the African bug with the instruments. It came out in a jiffy.

I showed it to Mr. Russell on a piece of gauze. The "bug" was about the size of a grain of rice. Though so tiny, it had reduced this tall, proud, stately man to his present sad condition.

"That's the bug, sir?" he whispered.

"That's it. It's a piece of scar tissue that formed where I removed the stitches from your lip after the operation."

He thought this over.

"Then there never was any African bug?"

"Just in your mind."

Slowly Mr. Russell rose to his feet. He seemed to have recovered his great height and his majesty of bearing. He spoke in the voice of a Jeremiah.

"Woman, woman!" he said. "See what I was, and see what you made me!"

Happily there was no worse ending than this, though there very well might have been. The sequel even persuaded me that, all things considered, the "African bug" I had unwittingly planted on Mr. Russell and the story of the outrageous fee I had told him to report to his uncaring love had worked out for the best. This sequel came in the form of a letter and a snapshot. In the letter Mr. Russell wrote that he had returned to his island home, Jamaica, and, as he said, "married the childhood sweetheart who remained faithful to me during my ill-fated venture in New York. You may consider, therefore, sir, that the words uttered in your office the last time I saw you were spoken in the warmth of the moment and have been withdrawn." In the picture he looked his true age, a handsome, smiling young man of thirty, with a smiling girl beside him.

"P.S.," he added in his beautiful Spencerian hand, quite in keeping with his speech and gravely courteous manner, "Emily declared at first sight of me that she did not care for the change; the new lip seemed to her pawky and ungenerous. She has since, however, as you will perceive in enclosed picture, reconciled herself to said lip. She joins her warm regards to mine."

And then a final paragraph:

"P.P.S. African bugs! Ha ha!"

Reading over his letter and looking at the picture of Mr. Russell, miraculously grown young again, it was impossible not to reflect that there are all kinds of "African bugs," some visible and some invisible; and that anyone who is the unhappy possessor of one will age before his time. These private, special, portable African bugs may be an unspoken fear, any old trouble or worry that has never been cleared up but buried away in the hope that gradually it would disappear. But of course it doesn't; it festers and grows worse. There is only one way to get rid of African bugs. The light of day is fatal to them. They must be brought out and exposed to it.

The Mystery of the Ballerina and the Smokeless Cigarette

FOUR OR FIVE YEARS PASSED. BY NOW I HAD TREATED A considerable variety of patients and flattered myself that I had acquired at least some degree of poise; but one afternoon I was given the experience of feeling as clumsy as a beardless interne.

Madame Nastasya Kirillovna had come in by appointment, and now sat in my consulting room with her beautiful legs crossed, a mink stole slung back from the fine shoulders, and a peculiar kind of cigarette stuck into her long jewelled holder.

At any rate the cigarette looked peculiar to me; I had never seen one like it before. Definitely it was not lighted; there was no ash, no smouldering spark, yet Madame Nastasya drew on the holder with every appearance of satisfaction and might have been inhaling great clouds of smoke when in fact there was nothing.

She awed me, but not because of the non-smoking cigarette. Even in repose she had an extraordinary air about her. You felt that if she wished to she could perform feats beyond human power, could rise from the chair in which she sat and float like thistledown before your eyes. That is the feeling a great dancer gives you, and Madame Nastasya was a very great dancer indeed.

She drew on the cigarette again, and again I had to restrain myself from getting up and offering her a light, which obviously she didn't want. "So, Doctor," she said, "how do I look to you?"

How would you answer such a question? Very nice, Madame—except for your face? For though the body was that of a girl, the face was marred by cheeks that had begun to sag and patches of soft, crepey skin.

"I mean, Doctor, how old? Forty-two or three?"

Yes, that's about what I'd have said, and I nodded.

"How much of that can you take off by this face-lifting business?"

The usual result, I told her, seemed to remove ten years from one's age.

"And you stay that way for how long?"

"You don't stay that way, you begin to age again. If you came in here a year after the operation, you'd look one year older. Face-lifting isn't anything fixed or permanent. It simply seems to take you back about ten years."

"Well, that's reasonable enough," Madame Nastasya observed. "When may I come in for the operation?"

"First we'll have to have an examination."

She made a moué of distaste. "Oh dear, an examination?"

"Just routine. Nothing to be concerned about."

"But after all, face-lifting isn't really a major affair, is it? Don't you just use local anæsthesia?"

"In most cases, yes."

"Why the examination then?"

It was puzzling that she should put up this objection. I tried to explain: "Well, for one thing, different people have different types of blood. Almost always you'll find that it coagulates normally, but there are exceptions and it's just as well to make sure."

"Oh," Madame Nastasya said, "*blood*," and smiled delightfully, dismissing it. "Well then, Doctor, let's have our examination right now."

But there proved to be more to it than that. The thing I

discovered about Nastasya Kirillovna, or thought that I discovered, was that she had a heart condition which even for a person leading a relatively inactive life could bring on an emergency at any moment.

At any rate so my stethoscope seemed to report. "I thought you said only blood, Doctor?" Madame Nastasya had protested when I brought it out.

"This will take only a second."

I had listened for a good deal more than a second, disturbed by that distinctive sound. Then I made some excuse and, leaving her in the examination room, I telephoned a friend in the building, a cardiologist. He came and applied his specialist's ear while Madame Nastasya regarded me with a smile I couldn't begin to fathom.

My friend took me off into an adjoining room and confirmed what I had suspected. "Mitral condition, perfectly well defined," he said. "Who's the exotic lady?"

"Nastasya Kirillovna," I told him. "The ballerina."

"The *what?*"

"Ballerina. You know, dancer."

"That's what I thought you said." He looked perplexed. Then his face cleared. "You mean that's what she *used* to be."

"Nothing of the sort. Didn't you read the rave reviews the other day about her performance in 'Swan Lake'?"

"Do you mean to tell me," said the cardiologist, "that this woman is actually dancing now?"

"Well, giving a mighty good imitation of it."

He grunted. "I suppose there are quicker ways of committing suicide but off-hand it's hard to think of one. She's lucky she came in to see you. Well, break it to her gently," and he nodded and left.

My glamorous patient was waiting for me, and she was still smiling in that odd way.

"Madame Kirillovna," I began, "the doctor who examined

you a few minutes ago is a cardiologist, a very good one, and he feels it would be wise if you arranged to have a complete——"

There she stopped me. "A complete heart examination."

"Yes."

"He suspected," she continued, taking up the funny cigarette again, "a case of—now let me think of those dreadful words. Yes, I have them. He suspected that I am the unhappy possessor of a mitral heart condition."

"How do you know?"

"Why, because I've been told so."

"You've been told so by a heart specialist?"

"Oh, by *dozens*."

"Then," I said, utterly taken aback, "what in the world is the idea of behaving like a lunatic?"

"Like a lunatic, Doctor?"

"If your condition has been diagnosed by dozens of cardiologists, as you say it has, then you know very well that you have no more business on the ballet stage than a one-legged man. Or are you trying deliberately to kill yourself?"

"I knew this was coming," Madame Nastasya sighed. "You must admit, now, Doctor, that I did my best to save us both from it. Really, you know, you misled me. You told me the examination would be perfectly routine, type of blood and other odd little things, and then without so much as a word of apology you whip out the fateful stethoscope, and we're in for it." She gave me a whimsical and reproving glance.

"Dear me, I do wish you didn't have to be so conscientious. Somehow I had the notion a plastic surgeon—particularly a *young* plastic surgeon—would be ever so much jollier and perhaps even rather devil-may-careish. Not like some horrid old German greybeard, Herr Doktor Wigglewoggleaufbauf." And she puffed out her cheeks comically and made deep tut-tutting sounds like an old gentleman with alarmist views.

"Madame Kirillovna," I said, "I don't understand any of

76

this, but if you are labouring under the impression that it's all very amusing, then I can assure you that it——"

"Isn't," she finished for me, with another sigh. "And now I see I've offended you. Oh, goodness!—and I suppose I'm to blame. I should have told you the truth in the beginning. Believe me, Doctor, please, I was only trying to spare you."

"You were trying to spare me what?"

"Trying to spare you all the painful thoughts you must be having now. I should have said——" For a moment or two she considered; then, indicating the jewelled holder, she went on: "I should have started in this way. Do you see this cigarette? Have you been thinking that it's a very strange one? Quite right. It's hollow, you see, except for the pellet in the mouthpiece end. The pellet contains a very strong spice. When you draw in on it"—and as she said this she lifted the holder to her mouth and inhaled deeply—"you receive the sensation that something is passing through your mouth into your lungs.

"Of course it isn't at all like tobacco smoke, it's only the palest imitation, and I wouldn't for a moment recommend it as a substitute to anyone who is in the heavenly position of not having to worry about what he does—but if you are a horrible, habitual, dyed-in-the-wool cigarette smoker, as I was, and your doctor orders you to give it up, well, then, this"—and she waved the imitation cigarette—"this is the next best thing!"

She regarded me quizzically.

"And that would have introduced you in an interesting, novel and painless way to the fact that my poor old heart is in a deplorable state, and would have spared us all the nasty business with your stethoscope and bringing your grim friend up to be shocked and dismayed too. Then I should have said, as I'm going to say now—Please, Doctor, don't think about my heart, don't think about me as a dancer. Think of me only as a vain female who wants to look ten years younger than she

77

is." She paused, then added in a lower voice: "Will you, Doctor?"

"You realize," I said, "that——"

"Yes," she interrupted quickly, "I realize that every time I step foot on the stage I'm taking my life in my hands, that I have no more business there than a one-legged man, as you put it (although, Doctor, I will not *altogether* agree with that!), and that I should give it up as I gave up cigarettes. Alas, there is no substitute. I realize that it is your duty as a physician to warn me of these things. All right, then, you have warned me, you have done your duty, and it's all finished with. Agreed? Or," she continued after a second of studying me, "are you afraid that the operation might be too much of a strain on my heart?"

"No," I said, "there's no danger there."

"A strain, then," she suggested, returning to her earlier, whimsical tone, "on your conscience?"

"Why should it be a strain on my conscience?"

She shrugged. "Operating on someone who isn't going to have much of an opportunity to enjoy the results of your work."

"I don't know why that should affect me."

"Dear Doctor," said Madame Nastasya, "I think you are an honest young man. I feel sure you don't like the idea of accepting money for something that may well be—phff-f-t!—over and done with in a week or a month or a year or two at most. Come, now, isn't that it?"

I didn't know how to answer her, and of course in my silence she read the answer. She gave a little laugh.

"I can put your mind to rest on that score. However short a time I have left, and whatever your fee may be, it will be cheap—because the circumstances are very special. So there, now, are we all settled? Or must we go on arguing for the rest of the morning? Do you give *all* your patients such a struggle, or am I the only one so honoured?"

78

She was the only one so honoured, for there had never been a patient like Nastasya Kirillovna before. I picked up the appointment book. "Next Wednesday morning," I said. "That means you'll enter the hospital Tuesday night. A week after the operation you should be ready to be discharged. Does that suit you, Madame?"

Madame Nastasya put away the jewelled holder and the absurd or perhaps one should say pathetic imitation cigarette. "Admirably," she said.

Face-lifting is not so much "lifting" as cutting away. The marks of age show most clearly in the crow's-feet wrinkles that gather beneath and around the eyes; in pouchy, rubbery folds that form under the chin; and in sagging cheeks. All these can be corrected by excision. The surgeon cuts out the aged, loose skin, brings the two edges of the wound together, and sutures them with extremely fine thread. Some days later the stitches are removed, and ultimately no evidence remains of the reparative work that has taken place.

The operation requires delicacy and skill, of course; so does anything involving a knife and human flesh; but the procedure is perfectly straightforward and seldom needs more than an hour and a half in the operating room.

Clad up to her neck in the sterile white gown, Madame Nastasya lay on the operating table and regarded me with calm eyes. She smiled, then closed her eyes against the tremendous sunburst of light from the globe overhead. After administering the anæsthetic—novocaine, injected into each section of the face as we came to it—the first step of the operation began.

The wrinkles around the right eye were rubbed away with the knife; then the left eye; then the right cheek and the left. In eighty minutes, more or less, we were finished. The bandages were applied and Madame Nastasya was wheeled down to her room in the hospital.

I stopped in during the evening to see how she was feeling. From the nurse's record I knew that there had been no complaints. Quite the opposite, said the nurse. "Gay as a cricket. A very fine patient indeed, Doctor."

To that I heartily subscribed. I had never seen anyone less affected by the atmosphere and paraphernalia of the operating room.

"Well, Madame," I said, "how are you? Any pain?"

"Not a bit. I'm so glad you came in—were you satisfied with the way everything went?"

"More than satisfied."

"So it's going to turn out all right?"

"It's going to turn out all right."

"I shall really look ten years younger?"

"You'll really look ten years younger."

She gave a sigh of what I took to be satisfaction and touched her bandaged face lightly. "I can't wait for all this to come off so I can see myself. When will it be, again?"

"Seven days," I said. "Until then, you'll just have to be patient."

I would have felt pretty well satisfied too had I been able to follow her instructions and forget that she was Nastasya Kirillovna the dancer, a woman who for reasons of her own seemed to be extending a cordial invitation to death, but of course I couldn't forget, it was impossible; and I began to wonder if, where so many others had failed—the specialists she had spoken of—I had any chance at all of persuading her to adopt a sensible view of her condition and adjust herself to the regime indicated for a heart cripple. At least I had a new approach, and this I determined to try to exploit for all it was worth.

On the seventh day after the operation I removed the last bandages and gave Madame Nastasya a hand mirror. The track of knife and sutures was still evident in the discoloured skin—another week or two would be required for it to dis-

appear—but where before there had been the pouchy patches
and the crinkled lines of crow's-feet there was now a youthful
smoothness.

She studied herself a long time, slowly turning her head
from side to side. At length she put down the mirror. "Thank
you, Doctor," she said. "May I leave the hospital now?"

"Whenever you wish."

"No instructions?"

"No," I said, "but I would like to——"

"Now," she interrupted, laughing, "no more 'Do-you-
realize-thats'!"

"No more 'Do-you-realize-thats'. Just a question. All right?"

"All right," she said, "that I grant you. Just a question."

"What are you going to do with yourself now?"

"Why, rest for a week or two at the home of some friends
of mine in the country. Then pick up where I left off."

"And where will that be?"

"Doctor, you said just one question," she reproved me, "but
I won't hold you to it, just so long as we manage to resist the
temptation of becoming all gloomy and conscientious again.
Why, picking up where I left off means with 'Les Sylphides,'
next month, the night of the twenty-second. And," she continued with her most delightful smile, "I should like you and a
friend to be my guests that night. It would give me great
pleasure to know that you are in the audience."

"Thank you," I said. "It'll be a pretty important night, I
suppose?"

"The night of any performance is."

"I mean, this one particularly?"

She raised her eyebrows in a quizzical look. "What are you
getting at now, Doctor?"

"After all," I said, "it'll be the unveiling of the 'new'
Kirillovna, won't it? The first time the audience will see your
new face."

"Why, yes," she admitted, "but none of them will realize

it. They couldn't possibly. So far as they'll know, it won't be a 'new' Kirillovna, but exactly the same one."

"Madame, I feel quite hurt," I said. "Here I'd been complimenting myself that we hadn't done too badly; but now you say no one in your audience will realize that anything's happened to you. I thought it would take a blind man not to see the difference."

"Of course anyone could see it!" she laughed. "But not anyone in a theatre audience. Think about this for a moment —when Sarah Bernhardt was seventy-nine or so, or maybe it was eighty-nine, she was playing the part of a seventeen-year-old boy, and no one in the audience burst out laughing. Not only because they respected her and loved her, but because she didn't look in the least ridiculous. You've forgotten that there's such a thing as make-up, which can perform miracles too. Particularly theatrical make-up. Soft lights, artful make-up—you never look your age, you always look just the same."

That was true. It destroyed the theory I had worked out.

I suppose she saw my face fall. "Now, let me see," she resumed. "I wonder if this isn't what you were after. You've been puzzling your head off about me, why I should want my face lifted in the present delicate state of my health; and it occurred to you that perhaps it was because I had set my heart on going out in a burst of glory—a sentimental, romantic and tragic occasion. Expire triumphantly, looking *exactly* to my last night's audience as I had looked when I first came to America, a young woman of thirty or so, ten years before." She paused for a moment. "Is that what you thought, my friend?"

I had to admit that it was. She gave a chuckle.

"No, you're way off. As I said, under the make-up it wouldn't make any difference if you'd turned me into a hag or a blooming damsel of sixteen." She fitted one of the tobaccoless cigarettes into her holder and waggled it back and forth while looking at me in a rather mocking, speculative way. "Would you *really* like to know why I had my face lifted?"

"Very much," I said.

"Then I'll tell you. It's nothing sensational; women always seem to be the same, alas. Ten years ago—no, it was eleven— I came over here on my first American tour, as I said. It was going to be my last. I was still young and I felt that I'd only begun to touch what I was capable of, but I'd fallen in love and was going to be married. That meant I must give up the dance; you can't give part of yourself to it and part of yourself to anything else, no matter what people say; not at any rate if you take your art seriously, and I do. I wasn't unhappy about it; I was too much in love.

"His name was Gerald. Yes, a young Englishman, of course; you'd know it from the name, wouldn't you?" She chuckled. "I'm English, too—you didn't know *that*, did you? There never was any Kirillov, doting husband of lovely, gifted Kirillovna—I won't tell you my real name, though, it's too much of a comedown. Kirillovna was just something we thought up, straight out of Dostoevsky. People simply refuse to believe you're any good as a dancer, you know, unless you're Russian. Actually, Gerald and I came out of very much the same kind of background and were brought up only about fifty miles away from each other, though of course we never knew it then.

"He was a darling. We'd met first at Cannes and it hadn't seemed to be anything earth-shaking; but then that mysterious something happened between us, and Gerald began to follow the company on our tour. I'll never forget the moment when he told me it was because of me. I told him that's what I'd been hoping he'd say. I'd had a fair share of attention, people running after me, but I'd always been insulated by my special world of the dance; I'd thought nothing would ever be able to reach through it and touch me. But Gerald did. Oh yes, Gerald did. He was so sweet, his skin was so fair, he had such

83

funny, thoughtful little ways about him, knew when to kiss me
and when not to, when to tell me a funny story and when to
shut up and hop it and leave me to do a bit of brooding, as
everyone has to once in a while. It just seemed that he knew
everything that was going on in my head. Well," Madame
Nastasya said after a moment's consideration, "*almost* everything.

"He was with us all through that first American tour and
everyone knew there was a special thing between us and they
were all very kind, even the manager, which was rather a
miracle. Then, almost the last night, indeed it may have been
the very last night of the tour—at any rate, whether it was or
not, Gerald turned up in my dressing-room, as he did after
every performance; but this time he had someone with him.
A girl.

"She couldn't have been more than nineteen. She was the
daughter of some American friends of Gerald's family and
she'd written and asked him if he'd give her the simply too
marvellous thrill of introducing her to me. You know, I was
on top of the world, the little thing looking at me adoringly,
and my darling there feeling very proud of me—at least so I
thought.

"But then—it was funny," Madame Nastasya said ruefully,
looking at me over the edge of the imitation cigarette, "it was
funny how it happened, the end of the world, just like that,
but very, very quietly. Just a whisper somewhere inside you,
'It's all over, dear, it's all finished.'

"Gerald didn't realize it himself and I knew we might go on
for weeks and months, but I'd only have been acting, waiting
for the time that I'd know was coming when he'd look at me
in a hangdog sort of way and say, 'I'm terribly sorry, old dear,
but somehow or other I believe I've gone and been foolish
enough to fall in love with little what's her name, you know,
the little girl I brought to meet you in your dressing-room that
night.'

"For it had really happened already," Madame Nastasya

84

went on. "I knew it but he didn't. Gerald had tumbled for her head over heels. And she was nineteen and I was thirty-one, and I knew how I looked beside her, there under the naked make-up table lights. Youth and age. Oh, not as bad as that, but that's how I felt.

"So I faced up to it and was fearfully brave and all that and saw what I had to do. Later on that night I told Gerald there was no getting around it, I'd discovered I couldn't leave my first love, the dance, not even for him. He was terribly upset at first but then, you know, I could see it slowly dawning on him: he was free, he was free to fall in love again wherever he wished; and I could see the thought of little miss what's her name slowly stealing into his mind.

"And that was that," Madame Nastasya finished. "Great romance all over. Back to the dance. And actually, do you know, it turned out to be all for the best. I don't think I really could have been the devoted housewife for very long, not even for Gerald; I would have had to go back to my real career. Give up cigarettes"—she made a grimace—"give up love, oh, yes, give up almost anything, but not *dancing*. I couldn't live without it. That's why it's all nonsense about my heart. I know *more* than the doctors, you see; if I had to stop dancing, then my heart *would* kill me.

"But be that as it may"—and now Madame Nastasya's voice took on a sharper tone—"I most certainly do not intend to have my precious Gerald saying to himself, 'Thank God we *did* bust up.' The little girl he fell in love with and married eleven years ago is thirty years old now, almost exactly the age I was when she stood with me there in the dressing-room and made me feel as ancient as the Sphinx. When Gerald sees us together this time, she'll look older, *but I won't*. This time all the advantage is going to be on my side, and Gerald is going to think, *Good Lord!—look at Nastasya there, young as ever; really makes poor Lucy look pretty seedy. I wonder if I did the right thing after all?*"

Madame Nastasya sat back in her chair. "And there's the whole story. That's why I'm so grateful to you, dear Doctor."

"So Gerald's going to see the two of you together again?" I asked.

"He is indeed."

"When?"

"The first night of 'Les Sylphides,' on the twenty-second— I've already sent you tickets, by the way. Gerald's going to be in New York then, with Lucy. I heard from him a few weeks ago and he said he'd seen that I'd be here then too and he thought it would be nice if the three of us met. So I wrote back and said I quite agreed, I thought it would be awfully nice, and why didn't he come backstage with Lucy to my dressing-room when we were finished and the three of us would go out and have a glass of wine somewhere and a nice chat."

"Then that was the real reason for the face-lifting."

"That was the real reason for the face-lifting." She chuckled. "What saith the prophet? Vanity, vanity, all is vanity."

"Well," I said, "I hope everything works out to your satisfaction."

"Goodness, Doctor, do you know that you sound disappointed? I suppose I shouldn't have said a word to you; or rather, I should have encouraged that lovely idea you worked up all by yourself, of the tragic, doomed Kirillovna who wished to die in a blaze of beauty." She waved the cigarette holder at me. "I'm afraid the facts of life are less romantic. Do you know what the sweetest thing in the world is? Getting back at some woman who's done you wrong. And that's precisely what I'm going to do."

I took my leave, a soberer and wiser man.

I went to the opening night of "Les Sylphides" with a friend who was a real ballet fan. I couldn't match his enthusiasm and adjectives, not owning his knowledge of the art; but it did seem to me I had never seen a purer expression of beauty than that slim, graceful figure which seemed to float around the stage.

At the intermission a page boy arrived with a note for me. "We're going to have a drink at Club 21 afterward," it said in firm, forward-slanting script. "Won't you join us with your friend? I should like it. N.K."

"By all means," I murmured. "Let us be in at the death."

"What?" said my friend.

"Madame Kirillovna has asked us to have a drink with her later on. Do you feel up to it?"

"Do I feel up to it?" he said indignantly.

"She won't be by herself."

"What does that matter? Just to sit at the same table with her!"

He was a tall, handsome fellow in his early thirties and I wondered if Nastasya might have taken a peep through the curtain hole and spotted him beside me and been inspired to send her invitation.

In any event, his eyes were full of stardust when we joined her at Club 21. I could see at once that everything was working out very much to Nastasya's satisfaction. Mrs. Gerald Spencer, the pretty little girl of eleven years ago, was now a washed-out blonde who looked nearly twice Nastasya's age; and it was obvious that her husband, poor Gerald, was kicking himself under the table for having lost the gorgeous creature laughing and smiling beside him.

Nastasya came in the next day for a final visit. "Well?" I said. "I suppose you enjoyed yourself last night?"

"Blissfully."

"You certainly rode roughshod over her. For the rest of your life you can lick your lips over the memory of how that pathetic little creature looked compared to you. I wouldn't give her one chance in ten of holding on to her marriage now."

"My dear Doctor," said Nastasya with a pitying smile, "obviously you'll never understand women. On the contrary, dear little Lucy will now have every chance in the world to hold on to her marriage, whereas before last night it was rapidly slipping away from her."

"What do you mean, she'll have every chance to hold on to her marriage *now?*"

"Why," said this extraordinary woman, "because for the next two weeks Lucy is going to be given the works at Elizabeth Arden's and Hattie Carnegie's, at my expense. When she gets through she's going to look as ravishing as she ever did, and Gerald will fall in love with her all over again. The dear little thing!" Nastasya said affectionately. "After what she did for me last night, making me feel so wonderful, could I do any less than show her how to make the best of herself too?"

Nastasya Kirillovna's experience would seem to recommend dancing as the proper treatment for a heart condition! But of course that isn't so. I do believe, though, that it was her devotion to her career that kept her alive, and that if she had slipped back into the role of an invalid she would have died.

Devotion to what she believed in. That is what seems to me Nastasya's essential and youth-preserving quality. Compared to this devotion, the episode with Lucy was merely an amusing little side-show.

The Blue Tattoo

QUITE A NUMBER OF YEARS AFTER KIRILLOVNA'S VISIT, another lady with a secret came to see me. She couldn't have been more unlike the dancer in appearance or manner and when I saw her first I would never have thought that here was someone I would remember, and remember vividly.

It was a smothering day in mid-August; the air didn't move; the people on the sidewalks gasped like fish; even the most vivacious cab drivers sulked. I thought long and earnestly of a Long Island beach and wished that I had cancelled my appointments for the afternoon.

The inter-office phone rang.

"Mrs. Marisius is here for her appointment, Doctor."

Still thinking about the Long Island beach, I put on my white jacket and went into the consultation room. This was Mrs. Marisius' first visit; she had made the appointment by telephone. The moment I saw her I forgot about the beach. A sedate middle-aged woman, Mrs. Marisius was extraordinary in her appearance in one respect: on this blistering day, when each additional ounce of clothing seemed to weigh a ton, Mrs. Marisius wore a long-sleeved dress. Nor was the material airy, diaphanous, as you would expect; it was good and solid.

Any doctor's eye and mind would leap to the proper deduction. Mrs. Marisius wore a long-sleeved dress of solid material because she would rather suffer from the heat than endure the curious or, possibly, shocked glances of passers-by. Obviously, either Mrs. Marisius' right arm or her left bore some kind of disfigurement.

But which arm, right or left? And how disfigured?

I saw that Mrs. Marisius favoured the right arm by keeping it folded across her lap, as if she had forgotten that she was wearing the protective long-sleeved dress. So it was the right arm that was marred. And it could be no small matter; something pretty dramatic. A bad burn scar, I fancied; for Mrs. Marisius' station in life was obviously that of the housewife, and about the easiest place in the world to run into a burn is the kitchen.

"Yes, Mrs. Marisius?" I said. "What can I do for you?"

She had a gentle voice. "You remove marks from people, Doctor?"

"Yes," I said.

"I have one on my arm."

I nodded.

"On my right arm, Doctor. Here, I'll show you."

She unfastened the clasp at the cuff and drew up the heavy sleeve.

But the angry red splotch of a burn scar I had expected wasn't there. Instead there was only a small blue stitching, deadly and evil as serpent's teeth, though at first I didn't understand its significance.

I bent forward to look at it. A letter and five figures stood out sharply against the soft skin.

T 38065

"How did you get that?" I asked.

"It was tattooed there, Doctor."

"Tattooed?"

"Yes; in one of the concentration camps in Germany."

Then of course I knew what lay behind the little blue legend. "I must have seemed very stupid to you," I said, feeling ashamed of myself in this small quiet woman's presence, as I realized what she must have suffered.

"Stupid?" she repeated. "No, no. Even though you knew about the Nazis, it is hard, here in America, to believe that human beings did these things to other human beings."

I asked her to tell me the story behind the blue mark, and after some persuasion she consented. The manner in which she told it seemed to dismiss her experiences as a routine tale of familiar events, perfectly routine and ordinary.

Mrs. Marisius' husband had been a doctor; to this fact she owed her life, just as in a sense he owed his death to it. Soon after the invasion of Poland, Dr. Thomas Marisius had been drafted for work in a medical research bureau connected with the Luftwaffe. He said nothing to his wife about this work but she assumed that its demands were heavy because he soon lost weight and stirred and talked much gibberish in his sleep, nightmarish words which the listening, worried woman could not understand. At length one evening he told her he had resigned from his post. She cried out how thankful she was. "It was killing you, Thomas!"

Dr. Marisius nodded sombrely. "It was," he said. "I wish I had had the courage to leave it before."

She did not altogether understand what he meant by this. Later in the night events began to make his meaning clear. The Marisiuses had four unexpected visitors, large, curt young men who got them out of bed, bade them dress and be quick about it, and hustled them off in separate cars with drawn curtains. Ilsa Marisius had hardly realized what was happening; her husband was bundled off before her eyes, a despairing look on his white face; he called out something but it made no sense, and the young men who thrust her forward into the second car would answer none of her questions.

Weeks later, in one of the concentration camps, a frightening place, she learned why the young barbarians had rooted them out into the night. A smuggled note came from Thomas. His

work in the Luftwaffe research bureau had been concerned
with experiments he still found himself unable to describe to
her. So, fearing the loss of his sanity or his life, he had quit.
But then they had seized Ilsa as a hostage. Thomas had been
forced to go back to work for their perverted science. As long
as he did, Ilsa would not be hurt.

"But be of good heart, Liebchen," the note concluded; and
there underneath was a little sign that might have been taken
for the cross mark indicating a kiss. In fact it was a secret signal
from the days of their courtship, meaning, Soon we shall be
together again.

Therefore Ilsa Marisius was of good heart.

In a few days another note was smuggled to her. She opened
it eagerly. The message was only one word, Good-bye.

Thomas and Ilsa Marisius had been married for thirty years.
Much as they had wanted children, they had never been given
any. So, now, after that one lonely, mortal word, Good-bye,
there was no point in living.

But then Ilsa considered all she knew about the men who
ruled her country. They were not stupid, they were clever.
They would never kill a doctor so brilliant as Thomas. They
had discovered his scheme to escape and get his wife out of the
camp, that was evident; but surely the word Good-bye did
not mean that they were killing him in punishment. Instead,
it must mean that they were sending him far off somewhere,
to work as a concentration camp doctor, perhaps in one of the
camps in the occupied territories.

So Ilsa picked up heart again.

If she was to live, she must pick up heart.

"Well, in those days you did not really live," she explained
to me now. "You just saw day in and day out. When I had
been considered a hostage they had not treated me too badly.
Now things were different. I was taken to another camp and
the number was tattooed on my arm. We were looked on as
working animals. No, I think that is too kind; animals are not

92

abused as we were. Those who thought they had something to live for, lived; those who had not, died. I thought I had something to live for—Thomas.

"Then finally one day it was finished; the gate was smashed in; a tank stood there, an American tank; and after a while I was free to look for my husband."

"You didn't find him?" I asked.

"No. But they had not killed him, the Good-bye had not meant that. Instead they had taken him to the very worst of the camps, to Belsen. I met a man who told me this. Thomas didn't last there long; he couldn't escape, it wasn't possible; on the other hand he couldn't go on doing what they made him do, and so"—and Ilsa Marisius shrugged—"he stuck the needle into his arm and died."

For three years she had been sustained by the conviction that Thomas was alive and waiting for their eventual reunion; for one year more she had searched for him. Well, now all that was over for good. She was very tired, she had seen much horror, she would be glad to die.

There remained only the question of how to kill herself.

But now troubles arose.

In this slaughterhouse, this executioner's block of a country, where there had been so much death—it proved to be extremely difficult to arrange for the death of one small, tired, fifty-year-old woman.

As a doctor's wife, Ilsa knew something about poisons. There was none to be obtained. Gas? The mains were blown to bits. She went to the top of one of the skeleton buildings; the masonry crumbled under her before she could jump and she was carried safely to earth in a dusty, rustling landslide of crumbled mortar.

But great trucks roamed the land, the trucks of the conquerors, the deliverers. At night, Ilsa crouched beside the road the trucks used. One of the monsters came roaring and grumbling through the darkness. Ilsa closed her eyes and stepped into its path.

The truck screamed like a dragon possessed, lurched off the road under the pull of the slammed brakes. The driver came bouncing out. "God damn it," he shouted, "just what in hell you think you're doing? You want to get yourself killed?"

This angry young American then gave Ilsa a fierce lecture about watching where she was going. She stared at him blankly. He returned to his truck and got it back on to the road. The monster started to lumber away, then stopped. The young driver got out again, this time more calmly. He came up to Ilsa and pressed something into her hands, then drove away for good.

She peered at her hands. The fierce young American had given her a chocolate bar and several packages of cigarettes.

And at that point Ilsa broke down, not in tears, not in laughter, but a mixture of both. For with the American boy's gift—and at that time in Germany chocolate and cigarettes were worth their weight in diamonds—suddenly she came to see herself as a ludicrous figure.

"It was an impossible contradiction," she continued. "It was comic, it was ridiculous. You struggled to remain alive, and were given the news of your beloved's death as a prize for winning. You struggled to die, you were given riches as a prize for failing. It wasn't only an ugly world, it was a crazy one; it had lost its mind in the blood and the terror; it was a grinning idiot. More than ever, I would have been glad to die, if only I could find a way!

"But then"—and here Ilsa Marisius paused and smiled, "then, do you know what I did, before trying still once more to kill myself? Something very simple, although at the time it seemed extremely complicated. I looked at the chocolate and the cigarettes in my hand and I was about to throw them away to show my disgust for this whole crazy world, but I thought no, that would only make me more ludicrous than ever. Do some-

thing *else*, do something *else*! Do what? What? The command
and the question were running around in my head and I felt
dizzy and angry and tired—and then, like a miracle, there was
the answer! Do what? Why, eat the chocolate!"

She clapped her hands together. "And I did! Every crumb
of it! And oh, dear Lord, how good it was! It had almonds
in it, do you know?—lovely fat plump almonds, buried in the
rich chocolate. I hadn't had anything as good as that to eat for
—how long?—oh, centuries and centuries. And as I swallowed
it all down, slowly, deliciously, there was another voice speaking to me inside my heart, not mine any more, someone else's,
and it was saying, 'Now, Liebchen, at last you're waking up,
you're getting your senses back, you're not being a stupid
goose any longer. Please go right on that way! Don't give
those dirty Nazi hounds the victory they could never win for
themselves: stay alive, Liebchen, stay alive! Repay the nice
American boy by staying alive! Do this for me, Liebchen,
please!"

Ilsa Marisius raised her eyebrows in a questioning, quizzical
look. "What was it? The effect of that lovely chocolate, that
unimaginable luxury, on a very, very empty stomach? I suppose so; but whatever it was, I seemed to hear Thomas speaking
to me, and—and, well, I did as he asked. The cigarettes? No,
I didn't smoke them, I sold them; and with what they brought
—a lot of money, you would be surprised—with this money
I bought food and clothes. And next I found a job, and a little
place to live.

"But the past was still all around me, and occasionally the
ugliness and the evil would drown the memory of Thomas'
voice. He would want me to cut the evil out of my new life
entirely, I knew. So I came to America. How simple that
sounds! It was not; it required the kindness of many, many
people. And now that I am here, there is only one thing to
connect me with the ugliness of the past." And Ilsa Marisius
pointed to the little blue tattoo on her arm.

During the operation, there came a moment when I was afraid she was going to faint. I couldn't understand why. There was no pain involved in excising the tattooed patch, it had been completely anæsthetized; and quite aside from that, was this a woman to flinch at anything? Yet I felt the sudden tenseness, heard the quickened breath; and I paused and asked her if everything was all right.

"Everything is fine, Doctor!" Ilsa Marisius assured me. "You mean, why am I carrying on so? Sheer emotionalism. Here, at fifty-two, I feel I am being born again!"

And as I completed the operation I could not help but think how many people grow old prematurely by building their own concentration camp out of grief and anguish that they persist in keeping alive.

The Little Old Lady with the
Seven-League Boots

I AM SURE I SHALL NEVER FORGET THE FIRST TIME I HEARD HER voice, like dainty music from long ago. I did not know the owner of this charming telephone voice but she said that she felt she knew me. It seemed that she had read a book of mine some weeks ago at her home in South Africa; and now that—much to her astonishment—she found herself a visitor in New York, she had been unable to resist calling me.

Very flattering. It was even more flattering to be asked if I would mind very much autographing the book for her.

"I'll be only too happy," I assured her. "Will you stop by here with it, Mrs.——?"

"Nesbitt, Doctor, Caroline Nesbitt. What time would be best for you?"

In a gush of fine feeling I asked Mrs. Caroline Nesbitt to tea that very afternoon.

I have said that Mrs. Nesbitt's charming voice made me think of music from another time; I expected her, then, to be —well, not young; and in this I was correct. Her hair was pure silver, and she was dressed in the dark, frilly clothes affected by many old ladies, almost Edwardian in their general effect of much lace and lavender water. But her face was surprisingly clear and her eyes had a bright searching youthfulness in their violet depths.

"Will you pour, Mrs. Nesbitt?" I asked her, indicating the tea service.

"But what a lovely room, Doctor!" she said, settling herself beside the tray. And the room too seemed to take on additional lustre from her presence; the wood panelling had a deeper, richer glow; the rugs seemed softer, finer; the pictures, the flowers, the silver teapot itself, all were touched with a new light.

"And so your home is in South Africa, I think you said, Mrs. Nesbitt?"

"Yes, Doctor, Cape Town. Two lumps or three?"

"Two please. A long way away."

"Isn't it, though! Really, do you know, I can still hardly believe that I am here, in this extraordinary city of yours. It almost sounds like a miracle."

I thought so too. It was difficult to think of her immaculate, fragile self moving through the great harsh modern world outside, in all that glare and blare of traffic and screaming voices and yelling headlines; it was remarkable, yes, it was a miracle that she had managed to find her way across all those thousands of miles and to be here, safe and sound. But then, she must have had companions, a loving family, to take care of her during the trip.

No, apparently she had come quite alone.

"It was a family matter, you see, Doctor," she explained. "I have a daughter here in New York and it's been so long since we saw each other last that I felt I really must pay her a visit."

"Is she your only child, Mrs. Nesbitt?"

"Oh, no, no!" She laughed gaily. "My only child indeed! I have four boys and three girls, Doctor, scattered all over the world. Thomas in Paris, Ronald in New Zealand, Charles in Winnipeg—I am going on to see him when I have finished here—and Arthur in London. And then the girls: Mary's in London too, Elizabeth's in Rio, and, of course, Antonia is here."

"A remarkable family," I commented.

"Well, naturally, *I* think so, although I do wish at times they had not all gone to such *remote* places. But then, really, I'm the remote one, aren't I, I suppose you'd say, off down there at the tip of Africa? Dear George—my late husband—moved there just after the war (no, not the last war, and not the war before *that*; the *Boer* War, Doctor, far too long ago for you to remember) and though I did my best to persuade him to come Home to England (we were engaged then, you see) my persuasions were not enough and I yielded to him instead. And I must say I am happy I did so. It is a lovely climate and our boys and girls were always the healthiest lot of youngsters a mother could wish.

"Of course when George died, twenty-five years ago that was now—goodness me, how time does fly!—I could have come Home but by then I was too attached to Cape Town and the house where I'd brought up my family, and so I stayed on. The children, of course, have all urged me, each one, to live with them, but somehow I—— Well, I'm fixed and settled and too old to change in my ways now.

"But look at me!" Mrs. Nesbitt declared ruefully. "How I am chattering on! And when it was the last thing in the world I intended to do! For I came here, of course, Doctor, in response to your very kind and thoughtful invitation, to talk about—not me, but you! Or, rather, your book, which I did *so* enjoy."

"It makes me very happy to hear you say so," I said.

"Really, I did so much! I thought to myself, Such an *interesting* life that young man has had—— Now, Doctor, don't look startled, you *are* still a young man, you know, as far as I'm concerned, for I'm old enough to be your mother. Yes, an interesting life, yet so sad, too."

"Sad?" I said.

"I mean," Mrs. Nesbitt explained softly, "the matter of—Sylvia."

"Oh, yes," I said.

"That all happened just as you described it in your book, Doctor?"

"Well," I said, "more or less."

"It was true that you met her when you went abroad to study at that hospital in Berlin?"

"Yes," I said.

"And you fell in love with her, this beautiful young American girl who was studying the piano in Berlin?"

"Yes."

"And she gave you reason to think that she—responded to your affection?"

"Well, yes."

"So much so, indeed, that you became—engaged?"

"Yes," I said.

"And you came back to America first, in order to establish your office and find an apartment, and you were to be married when she—joined you?"

I nodded.

"But instead," Mrs. Nesbitt continued very gently, "Sylvia —gave herself—to another?"

"Yes," I said.

Mrs. Nesbitt sighed. "Poor boy, how you must have suffered. At that age a broken romance is such a dreadful blow; it seems like the end of the world. Oh, yes, I know what I'm talking about, because a mother, Doctor, with seven children growing up and falling in love and out of love—a mother knows. For that matter, in my *own* experience, when I was just a slip of a girl, before I met George—there was a certain singer, all the rage at that time in London—I shan't mention his name and anyway it would mean nothing now, although he used to be so famous that do you know there was a cigarette named after him?—and a very good cigarette, too, or so I was told, for of course in those years no decent young woman would dream of touching her lips with tobacco—but at any rate, oh what a crush I had on him, and had reason to believe, too, that he was not—what shall I say?—not *indifferent* to me—and then, when he married this heiress, goodness me, the torments I suffered! Another cup of tea, Doctor?"

"Thank you," I said.

"Two lumps, I believe?"

"Two," I said. "Thank you."

"So, you see, I am familiar with these things," Mrs. Nesbitt continued, having poured and given me the fresh cup of tea. "But usually, of course, with the freshness and optimism of youth, one soon recovers, the broken heart is magically mended. And, you must confess, it was true in your case too —wasn't it?"

"Well, of course," I said, "I didn't exactly——"

"I mean to say, Doctor, you—found another? And lost your heart—again?" Mrs. Nesbitt took a delicate sip of tea and gave me a look of such charming piquancy that it might have come from a sixteen-year-old girl.

"Well," I said, "I——"

"Yet," Mrs. Nesbitt said, "if I read your book correctly, and I am sure I did, for I simply *dwelt* on every word, it was all so fascinating to me—yet you never—married?"

"Well, no," I said.

"Then you were, were you not, remaining true to the memory of—Sylvia?"

"It wasn't exactly that," I said.

"Do you mean that somehow or other the right girl did not come along?"

Mrs. Nesbitt would pause a little, as I have indicated, before the final word of each of her questions. The effect was one of great delicacy and archness.

"I suppose you could say that," I said.

"So I thought to myself," said Mrs. Nesbitt. "A doctor's busy life—I have observed that if he does not marry at the beginning of his career, when he is just setting up in practice— as, indeed, you intended to marry, Doctor, if Sylvia had not disappointed you—if he doesn't marry then, he finds himself caught up in the rush and hurly-burly of his work, and somehow the opportunity or the inclination doesn't come along again. And what a pity! How many perfectly wonderful marriages and lovely families must have been lost in this way! For who can make a better father than a doctor? And who, more than a doctor, needs a partner in life, to look after him? Really, don't you—agree?"

"I suppose so," I said.

"Yet the poor man simply hasn't the chance to look around and find the right girl! So immersed in his work, to the exclusion of everything else—yet no, how stupid of me! Here I am virtually holding your book in my hand!—yet I said immersed in his work to the exclusion of everything else! Of course, you have your *writing*, too. Yet, on second thought, that rather contributes to the same end—doesn't it?"

"I'm not sure I follow you, Mrs. Nesbitt," I said.

"Wrapped up in your medical work, and on top of that wrapped up in your writing, I am sure you have had even less chance than the average doctor to look around and find that certain girl who will make the perfect life partner—isn't that true?"

I did not attempt to answer this question. An extraordinary suspicion was beginning to form itself in my mind.

"Well, of course, Mrs. Nesbitt," I said, "not everyone can feel confident that his marriage will work out as well as yours did. Seven children you said, didn't you? And by now I suppose you've a fair number of grandchildren too?"

"Indeed I have!" my small, frail guest replied enthusiastically. "There are Thomas's two and Ronald's three and Charles's one and Arthur's two—and the girls': Mary's three lovely daughters, and Elizabeth's fine twin boys."

"That's only six," I said, for I had been careful to count.

"Six, Doctor?" Mrs. Nesbitt laughed. "No, no, twelve; you miscounted. Twelve grandchildren in all—*so* far."

"I mean," I said, "six *children*. You said you have seven children, four sons and three daughters. But in telling me about *their* children, you only listed your four sons and two daughters. You left out one daughter."

"Of course I did," said Mrs. Nesbitt. "Antonia."

"Yes, that's right," I said. "Antonia. Isn't she the one who's living here in New York?"

"Indeed she is!" Mrs. Nesbitt replied as enthusiastically as before.

There was a slight pause.

"Then, Mrs. Nesbitt," I continued, "why didn't you count Antonia's children too?"

"Why," said Mrs. Nesbitt, "because she *hasn't* any. For some reason or other—and such a charming girl she is, so attractive, if I do say so, and, would you believe it, interested in writing too, as you are—for some reason or other Antonia has never found the right—man!"

She put down her teacup.

"And really, Doctor, before I leave New York, I simply must see to it that the two of you meet. You will find you have *so much* in common!"

At least it was easy to think of an inscription for the book, when Mrs. Nesbitt remembered that that had been the reason for her call. Or at least the announced reason for her call.

When she was "finished" in New York, as she had said earlier, she was going on to Winnipeg, to see her son Charles. Then she thought she would drop in on daughter Mary in London. Then next year there would be daughter Elizabeth to see, in Rio de Janeiro, and son Ronald in Auckland, New Zealand.

For it seemed that Charles's son and Mary's daughters and Elizabeth's twin boys and Ronald's two boys and one girl were reaching good ripe marriageable ages.

In fact, I had in front of me, in the person of the gentle,

charming, frail-seeming little Caroline Nesbitt, one of the most redoubtable, unquenchable, indomitable matchmakers of all time.

And I had marvelled that she had managed to find her way across all those thousands of miles, in the blare and scurry of the modern world!

Secure on those tiny, delicate feet were a pair of hundred-league boots that would carry little Mrs. Nesbitt swiftly and surely as an arrow to her target when she scented a new match to be made.

I wrote in the book:

To Caroline Nesbitt
With profound admiration

As a postscript I must add that Antonia, the unmarried daughter, turned out to be profoundly suspicious of her mother's activities. We never met, and this remarkable match, conceived in South Africa and pursued half-way around the world, came to nothing. But to Caroline Nesbitt I owe the memory of a person who, perhaps more than anyone else I have ever met, *kept her eye on the ball*—which to me explained her youthful face and the liveliness and cheerfulness shining in her eyes.

The President, the Gasolina,
and the Silent Woman

AN INVITATION ARRIVED ONE DAY TO VISIT SEVERAL CENTRAL American universities and hospitals and lecture on some of the new techniques in plastic surgery, demonstrating these methods in the operating room.

My first stop was at Managua, the capital city of Nicaragua. A group of patients were waiting in the patio of the General Hospital. There was a girl whose lip seemed to split in two when she smiled (so of course she almost never smiled; her face was usually a sullen downcast mask). There was a man whose chin was pinned to his chest by a burn scar; half a dozen children with grotesque malformations; and finally a brother and sister, the boy eight, the girl ten, who in one respect were twins: each had been born with a hare-lip.

These people had been waiting for an hour or two and had undergone all the boring but necessary interviews with the hospital authorities before we arrived, so they—children and parents—were understandably impatient.

"Finally! Thank God!" one of the children shouted when the group of doctors at last appeared.

The brother and sister with the hare-lips were last in line. One never thinks of children as being exactly anxious to face the surgeon's knife; well, you should have seen these Nicaraguan youngsters. They were not worried about the operation; they were only worried about whether we'd get to them. The girl was standing behind her brother but now she darted in front. "Me!" she declared. "I should come first! Because look, everybody!"—and she pointed to that pathetic lip— "Look! Mine is bigger than his!"

"It is not!" the brother shouted indignantly. "Por Dios, what a liar she is! Any fair-minded person would have to grant that mine is far bigger!"

Here their mother took a hand and tried to quiet them but only a bigger uproar resulted until it was explained that everyone, whatever the size of his or her hare-lip, was going to be taken care of before the day was finished.

"Everyone?" repeated the mother dubiously.

I said as earnestly as I could, "Both, *Señora*, believe me." She bowed her head a little and turned away and then turned back, clasped her hands and began to sing. This was, I thought, a strange way to show her gratitude, for her voice was cracked and off-key. Then I recognized the song. It was "The Star Spangled Banner."

"A long day's work, Doctor," the chief of staff of the hospital commented some seven hours later. "Will you join me in a cigar and a glass of wine?"

I thanked him but was bound to refuse, for I'd have to hurry if I was to keep my engagement for the evening; this, I explained, was with the President, who had graciously invited me to a dinner at the presidential palace.

"Well," said the chief of staff, grinning, "you're in for an experience, all right. Are you a good listener?"

"Pretty fair. Why?"

"You'll find out!"

Walking through the patio on my way to the car, I noticed a woman standing in the shadow of one of the pillars. It was impossible to miss her because, though dressed in the typical humble costume of the farm woman, she had a rare beauty about her and an aristocratic way of carrying herself, as if she wore not her toil-stained clothes but plumes and ermine. Her eyes met mine for a second, then I passed on and emerged into the steaming bath of the late Managuan afternoon and was caught up by the sights and sounds of the streets—a wedding procession, a funeral, side by side; the merchants and pedlars and beggars; a huge man on a little wheeled platform pulled by a goat; women with baskets of fruit balanced on their heads; colour and noise and smells, and above all the drenching heat. Then we came to the hotel and the blessed cool water of the shower.

At the proper time I presented myself at the presidential palace. It was a very magnificent affair. So was the president; his splendour staggered the eye. He was a one-man pageant, a kind of Latin American Henry the Eighth, with great jolly cheeks, an enormous paunch and a balancing protuberance behind. The weight of gold he carried was incredible; a veritable museum of medals and decorations adorned his chest; his shoulders were a carnival glory of epaulets; and smack across the front of him ran a blazing red ribbon.

I was placed next to him at dinner and speedily discovered what my friend the hospital chief of staff had been hinting at. For the president liked to tell funny stories; and tell them he did, old friends from all over the world, Pat and Mike and the Scot who reported on the dreadful expense of visiting London, first ten minutes I was there, bang went sixpence; who was the lady I seen you with last night, that was no lady, that was my wife—an ambulatory Joe Miller's Joke Book.

But at least you weren't put to the trouble of producing a properly hearty imitation laugh; the president would never have heard it, he laughed so uproariously himself, and slapped his mighty thighs with blows that would have felled an ox.

It was a long, long evening but at last it neared its end. "Sir," I said, "I have been told that you own an extremely beautiful parrot. May I see it?"

The president nodded. "By all means!"—and took me by the arm.

We went through one magnificent chamber after another

and then came to the most splendid of all, a sumptuous room, intended no doubt for the grandest occasions of state, with polished floor and huge windows and mirrors and elaborate draperies.

"There she is," said my host. "Come, Estrellita, darling, say something for the gentleman, won't you, my pretty flower?"

In the middle of the dais at the end of the room stood a bird cage on a golden stand. A strange object occupied the cage.

"Well?" the president inquired. "You must confess, now, that the advance description hardly does her justice?"

Here the object in the cage cocked its head and fixed me with a baleful stare. It was a bird, yes, but so ancient that it resembled a fossil rather than a bird. Absolutely nude, without the trace of a feather, shrivelled and wrinkled, the bare skin a leaden blue colour, it reminded me of an evil little old man.

"A beauty, eh?" chortled the President, slapping his thigh again. He leaned closer, heaving and wheezing. "She is extremely sensitive," he whispered, "as delicate as a maiden, and unless you say something complimentary to her she mopes and pines all day. Please, tell her something."

I could think of nothing to say.

"Well, then," he went on, "I'll give you a tip, the phrase she dotes on above all others. Say this to her, '*Señorita*, will you be mine? *Señorita*, will you be mine?'"

I went up to the cage. "*Señorita*," I said with a shudder, "will you be mine?"

The hideous fowl raked me from head to foot with its evil stare. "You loafer!" it screamed. "You impudent no-good! I'll have you know I'm a decent and honourable girl! I'm decent and honourable, I am!" And standing upright on the perch she flapped those grotesque leathery stumps of wings in a paroxysm of fury.

So ended the evening.

But odd though his taste in humour was, the president was

as good as his word when it came to the arrangements he had promised to make for the rest of my tour through Nicaragua. Two days later, promptly on the dot of eight, Colonel de la Mora, who was to be my escort, called for me at the hotel and drove me to the railway station. Since the train for the town of Granada was not scheduled to leave until the afternoon and I was anxious to spend the whole day there, the president had decreed that the apple of the railroad's eye, the vehicle called the *Gasolina*, should be brought out for my exclusive benefit.

The *Gasolina* was a small car about eight or nine feet long, navigated by a tall, gloomy youth who seemed to have sore gums, for he sucked them continuously. Starting the gasoline engine, he drove us off at a furious clip, soon leaving the swarms of yapping dogs behind; and an hour and a half later, a bit breathless but still intact, we arrived at Granada, fifty-five miles away.

Here we were greeted by a medical group headed by the elderly dean, a charming, courtly old gentleman, who had studied in New York at Bellevue. Taking us to the hospital, he introduced me to my patients. Among them was a young Army captain, badly scarred by a bullet that had passed through both left and right cheeks, leaving a mark that never permitted him to forget the revolution in which he had suffered it, though everyone else had long since forgotten. There was also a lawyer, or rather an ex-lawyer, who had lost his practice due to an unfortunate marital mix-up in which he had mistaken another woman for his wife and, since the lady was engaged in amorous dalliance, slashed at her with a knife—and, in return, had been carved up by her friend. The lawyer had served his jail sentence but the scars remained to remind every-one of his hot temper and suspicious mind.

Next came a boy with webbed fingers; another hare-lip; and three burn scar cases. The distinguished-looking old dean had a glass of chilled pineapple juice ready for me when I had

finished washing up; I drank it, thanked him and the rest of
the staff and hurried off to the waiting *Gasolina*—it was nearly
five o'clock now and, remembering some of the things I had
seen on the way up, the cows and goats wandering across the
railway tracks, I was not enthusiastic about the prospect of
travelling back to Managua through the tropical night.

Coming down the hospital steps I was struck by a face that
seemed familiar but I could not identify its owner until the
Gasolina was well under way. A woman, dressed in peasant's
clothes, but with a singular air of dignity. Then I knew who
she was: the same woman I had seen three days ago in the patio
of the General Hospital at Managua. It was something of a
coincidence that I should come across her at each place just
after finishing the day's operations.

The *Gasolina* galloped on, although that is not really the
proper way to describe its raucous progress over the rails, with
engine blatting loud and the gloomy driver industriously suck-
ing his gums. One moment the pale hot light of late afternoon
lay around us; the next, a curtain might have dropped.

Our pilot caused the *Gasolina* to emit a melancholy hoot,
then he kindled its headlight, which had the immediate effect
of turning the vehicle into a small Juggernaut. Swarming into
the headlight's glare, bugs by the million began to immolate
themselves. It was impossible to see, to be conscious of anything else. Colonel de la Mora and I pulled our collars up
around our necks and stuck our heads down between hunched
shoulders; and so, presumably, did our gum-sucking navigator; for the next thing we knew, with no warning, no shout
of alarm, no attempt to apply the brakes—there was a great
rending *thump*, a succession of horrible sounds, and the impression of huge wrathful bodies hurtling back and forth in the
mysterious night. The crash had put out the headlight but
eventually de la Mora and I untangled ourselves; somehow he
found a flashlight and we were able to survey the scene.

It was a grisly one. The survivors were still hastily departing, but two or three had fought their last fight and would never leave the field. They had, however, left their mark.

We had smashed full-tilt into a herd of cows.

The *Gasolina* sat inert on the rails, uttering no sound except a feeble internal ticking. After a long, long period of probing into its vitals, the engineer announced he had discovered what the trouble was.

"Good," de la Mora said impatiently. "Then fix it, boy, and let's be on our way."

"Ah, sir, but it cannot be fixed," said the youth. "It is the carburettor, sir, and no one could fix it, it is shattered beyond repair. Only one thing will suffice."

"And what is that?" the colonel demanded testily.

"A new carburettor, sir, which of course I do not have, for who would have foreseen that these beasts would hurl themselves at us so savagely?"

Well, then, what could be done?

We had a choice, the youth informed us; wait where we were or start to walk along the tracks, either way, it made little difference, for he estimated that we were equidistant from Granada and Managua. For himself, he intended to wait; the morning train from Granada would be along in another seven or eight hours. And with a smile, the first I had seen on that lugubrious face, he curled himself up and went to sleep.

De la Mora and I looked at each other. Sit or walk? It was a matter of indifference to the mosquitoes whether we elected to offer them stationary or moving targets. We decided to sit. It was impossible to sleep (the gloomy youth apparently possessed an impregnable hide), and so we talked. The colonel told me about his army career and I in turn described the operations I had performed during the day and ended up by telling him about the woman I had seen both at the hospital in Managua and now in Granada. "Funny coincidence, isn't it?" I said.

"Funny?" said the colonel. "Not at all! You have made a

conquest, my friend! She is following you around because you have captured her heart. Ah! When you see her next—speak to her!"

"That's ridiculous," I said.

"Ridiculous? You do as I say!"

Much swollen, red-eyed and weary, we were rescued by the morning train, which pushed the *Gasolina* ahead of it and brought us to Managua. We spent two days recuperating and then—in a repaired and presumably chastened *Gasolina*, with a different engineer, an elderly, cautious man—we started off for the third town on our tour, Leon, forty miles or so down the tracks in the other direction.

The hospital we were to visit had been founded by the famous Dr. de Beyle, who almost single-handed had brought modern medicine to Nicaragua years before. He had fought an uphill struggle that many another would have despaired of, facing age-old superstition and ignorance.

Perhaps his most depressing experience came with the discovery that these tendrils of superstition reached into his own home.

His young bride of several months would never leave the house on a cloudy night.

Why not? the doctor asked.

Why, because pregnant women should never look at the moon when clouds were passing over its face; better to stay at home and not take the chance.

De Beyle's hackles rose, and on the next cloudy night he insisted that his wife step outside, and he himself would see to it that her eyes were wide open.

"Very well, *Señor*," said the lady, "but you will regret it."

A few months later Dr. de Beyle was the proud father of a baby boy. A fine son in every respect—well, almost every respect. The infant's right cheek was marred by a strawberry blotch the size of a penny piece. It was not the birthmark that distressed the father; it was the quiet, meaningful look his wife gave him, as if to say, "So, *Señor*, you see? You and your modern science! *Now* perhaps you will believe what I say about looking at the moon on a cloudy night?"

But that was a long time ago. Now here we were chugging into the Leon station and pulling up before the welcoming committee, led by his honour the mayor. A brass band, very grand in blue and yellow uniforms, blasted away in the background and drowned out his honour's official greeting; but that didn't matter—we had our own private greeting, established years before.

A handsome young man, the mayor beamed down at me. "Please tell me, *Señor* Doctor," he quavered, imitating a little boy who is trying to be brave but cannot resist the question, "please tell me—*will it hurt?*"

For this was Roberto de Beyle, the moon-struck child, whose birthmark I had removed when his father had brought him to New York twenty and more years ago.

Among the cases assembled at the hospital were three of exceptional interest: the first, an eight-month-old baby girl who had been born with three distinct nostrils; the second, a boy whose face was separated into two halves by a flaring birthmark that would have put Roberto de Beyle's to shame; and an elderly gentleman who reminded me of my old friend Mr. Cremona, the barber of my boyhood days back on Attorney Street. The old man's jaw was disfigured by an ugly growth that he wished to have removed.

"Don't be offended," I said, "but why is it important to you to have it done now, when you have lived with it for so long?"

"*Señor*," he replied with great dignity, "I did not come into the world with it, and I wish to leave the world as I entered it; that, I think, is the least I owe my Maker, in whose image we are all made."

I left the hospital at the end of the day deep in talk with a group of doctors and was getting into the waiting car when something caused me to glance back. And there she was, the same woman! Now this had gone beyond coincidence and I could not help recalling what de la Mora had said. Absurd, of course, and yet—well, there was no getting around it; I felt pleasantly thrilled. This beautiful dark-eyed woman had actually journeyed back and forth all that distance, from Managua to Granada, from Granada back to Managua, from Managua down here! I touched the driver on the shoulder and asked him to turn back; and at the hospital steps, I got out of the car. At least I should say something to her.

Her head bowed, she was walking away. I caught up with her. Smiling, I said: "I've seen you two or three times now, and I wondered—well, shall we shake hands?"

She took my hand. With her other hand, slowly she opened the blouse she was wearing.

And then she guided my right hand to her naked breast. I drew back, but she insisted.

An ugly lump was growing in the soft flesh.

Now, not only was this woman illiterate; we found also that she had been born without the power of speech. She had no knowledge of doctors or of hospitals. We could only surmise —after the breast cancer had been safely removed—that someone had pointed to me and told her I was a Norte Americano who had come here to remove bad things from people's bodies. And so she had followed us from town to town.

I am sure that is the reasonable explanation. There is another. Some years before, my mother had died of cancer of the breast. The woman in Nicaragua did not know what it was that was growing in her breast; she only knew it was evil.

Had something whispered to her, "Show him. *Show him*"?

Why else, that night, did I dream of the old home, and mother, smiling?

But whatever the truth, I know one always feels at his best —young and alive—when he has helped someone else.

The Strange Case of the Ugly Duchess

AT OUR NEXT STOP, THE HOSPITAL OF SAN JUAN OF GOD, IN Costa Rica, the doctor who made the greatest impression on me was Tomas Rodovaldes.

And there were some striking individuals on the staff. For example, the director of the hospital, who had installed a time clock and prided himself on being the first one to punch it every morning. One day he was beaten to the clock by a colleague. He immediately ruled that the clock had suddenly developed some mysterious inner malady, making its records for the morning worthless.

This story was told to me by the chief surgeon, with a chuckle at his friend's quirk; and as I listened I couldn't help noticing that he, the chief surgeon, wore a wig.

I was introduced next to the eye specialist on the staff, who apologized for his faulty English; he explained that he had only recently taken up its study.

"But wait!" he declared confidently. "Five, seex months from now, you weel see—I weel speak heem better than Shakespeare!"

But Dr. Tomas Rodovaldes seemed nervous and uneasy. I couldn't understand why; I thought everything had gone off well during the day.

We had arrived early in the morning by plane; beneath, the city of San José had looked scrubbed white in the sparkling young sun; as for the hospital, it was immaculate. Founded a hundred years ago as a modest establishment with twenty beds, the Hospital of San Juan of God now boasted twelve hundred, and had no less than eight operating rooms.

Colour met your eyes everywhere: the patio was a small sea of flowers, the nurses wore uniforms of a pastel lavender shade; and each had an orchid pinned to her breast. I saw only one lonely speck of dust all day, and that for no more than a second —a porter, also clad in lavender, darted past me with a mop and attacked it like a dragon.

In the children's ward, one of the patients, a boy of nine or ten, was overcome by the sight of the phalanx of doctors suddenly descending on him, and plunged under the bedclothes. All our entreaties failed to lure him out. Then the doctor who had apologized for his English bent over and whispered a few words. As if by magic the little boy popped out and slowly held his right hand up for my inspection. The second and third fingers were webbed. "We'll soon have that fixed," I said, and, consumed with curiosity, turned to the magician. "What did you say to get him to come out?" I asked.

He gave a shrug and a wink. "Ah, it was nothing," he said. "They show the movie pictures in the wards, you know? And yesterday everybody was seeing Weenston, you know, Weenston Churchill? And so, you understand, everybody here is imitating heem. So I say to our young friend here, 'Pay attention now,' I say, 'for this doctor who has come to see you is going to fix your hand so *you* can make V for Victory sign too!'"

This and other incidents combined to make me feel thoroughly at home, with old friends—but as I have said, Tomas Rodovaldes was the exception. He stayed on the outskirts of the group, and at lunch, a wonderfully good-humoured meal, he joined in none of the talk and stories and laughter but kept his eyes on his plate, nervously crumbling a bit of bread between his fingers. I was puzzled by this tall, spare, handsome man's conduct but could hardly inquire into it.

We put in a busy afternoon with a great array of what might

be called "passionate" scars, all produced by affairs of passion: a lady who tackled her rival with a razor blade, only to discover that the other was similarly armed; two men who had had it out with machetes; and various other stabbings, with a few gunshot scars thrown in.

You could not have been blamed for coming to the conclusion that Costa Rica was a very hot-blooded country indeed, but of course the evidence was misleading. These patients had been gathered together in a special group for my visit. Their scars were not the product of a week or a month but of years.

Now, at the end of the day, having washed up and changed my clothes, I was waiting for the car that would take us back to town. The evening shadows were climbing up the mountains that rimmed the horizon. As I wondered what strange things you might find back in that high, distant land, a white-clad figure approached me in the dusk, coming out of the passageway that led to the hospital's chapel. It was Tomas Rodovaldes.

The director of the hospital and a few others were to meet me for dinner in a couple of hours; on impulse I asked Dr. Rodovaldes to join us. For the first time, he spoke to me.

"That is very kind of you, Doctor; unhappily, I am otherwise engaged. But"—and he hesitated, then gave a little nod, as if to himself, and went on—"but would you give me the pleasure of joining me for a drink right now? There is a café not far from here that I think you might enjoy."

At the café to which we went the nervousness of the day left him and Tomas Rodovaldes became as charming in manner as he was handsome in appearance. We talked about various things; then there came a pause; and I saw that again he had fallen back into his nervous habit of crumbling a piece of bread between his fingers.

"Did you ever hear of the Ugly Duchess, Doctor?"

"The Grand Duchess Marguerite?"

117

He nodded. "Marguerite, that was her name. Marguerite, with the face of a gargoyle."

I remembered an old picture of this unhappy fifteenth-century noblewoman, ruler of a small German duchy. The face of a gargoyle, Rodovaldes had said; it was no exaggeration—the forehead was low, apelike; she had great pouches under the eyes, and the lips were puffed and protruding.

"Poor woman," I said. "Yes, Doctor, I remember very well."

"We have an Ugly Duchess here," said Dr. Rodovaldes.

I waited for him to go on. He had pulled the bread to crumbs and now sipped nervously at his glass.

"I was waiting for her to come to the hospital to-day," he said. "I wasn't supposed to say anything about her to you. She didn't wish me to use my influence as a medical colleague in her behalf—as it was to be up to you to decide about her, quite by yourself. You see, she is extremely shy, painfully self-conscious—God knows, she has reason to be—and because she has suffered so much herself, she refuses to try to gain favours at the expense of others."

"You seem to know her very well," I ventured.

"Quite well. She's my sister."

He put his glass down and met my eyes directly.

"You must have thought I was behaving very strangely to-day. It became a matter of considerable tension to me, waiting for her to appear. Had she come there, Doctor, it would have represented a great victory, a victory of Angela—that's her name, of all names in the world!—a victory of Angela over Angela: to have come out and faced the world, which she ran away from years ago."

"But she didn't come?"

"She didn't come, and I haven't heard from her. We have a farm up in the mountains, you see; Angela and I grew up there. Of course I knew she didn't look like other little girls, but the only children around us were those of the farmers who worked for my father, gentle peasant children who treated Angela with respect and courtesy. Then it came time to come down to the city to go to school.

"I remember that first morning. We were walking along the street with a servant; it was like a nightmare, for out of nowhere a crowd of hooting, howling ragamuffins gathered, throwing dirt and filth at Angela. The servant chased them off; 'all these city brats are like that,' he said—but Angela wasn't deceived, she knew and I knew the real reason, her face, that grotesque, ridiculous, pathetic face. . . . She went back to the farm, and she has stayed there ever since."

I was thinking about the Ugly Duchess of history. If she had lived in the twentieth, instead of the fifteenth century; what could have been done for her? Despite the tales of miracles one hears, and the remarkable deeds sometimes performed in motion pictures, you cannot change one face into a completely new face. The plastic surgeon is limited by the basic structure —but as least a very substantial improvement could have been effected, the pendulous lips reduced in size, the sagging jowls removed; and if Angela resembled the Ugly Duchess, this could be done for her.

"When may I see her, then?" I asked.

"That is the problem," Dr. Rodovaldes said. "Obviously she lost her fight with herself to-day. When I realized this, I felt greatly depressed. Then I stopped for a moment in the chapel and it became clear to me that I was behaving very foolishly. My sister needs a hand held out to her, whereas I was standing back and letting her go through the struggle all by herself. Instead, I should go to her. That is, if you will go with me.

"When you see her in the surroundings to which she is accustomed it will not be so hard or painful for her. There won't be all those curious, scornful, jeering eyes around her. And you will be able to tell us what can be done, if there is any hope at all. The question is, can you spare the time? Would you be willing to take the whole day to-morrow and come with me up into the mountains, to our farm?"

I told him I was anxious to go, and Tomas Rodovaldes gave me a courteous little bow.

The next morning, in his car, we were soon out of town and climbing towards the great backdrop of mountains massed across the horizon. In half an hour it was possible to feel a definite change in the air as the road rose steadily, unfolding new panoramas of tilled fields, neat farmsteads, and seemingly limitless rows of coffee bushes. The better grades of coffee, Rodovaldes informed me, were grown in the uplands, the cheaper grades below; the colder, cleaner air apparently affected the exotic bean much as it was affecting me at this moment: I felt full of life and vigour.

Now, seeming to grow by magic out of its surrounding peaks, the great hunched spire of the volcano Irazu loomed up.

"In the bad old days," said Rodovaldes, "human sacrifices had been made to Irazu; and," he continued wryly, "it still gets its taste of blood. Half a dozen times a year some poor soul will make his way up there and throw himself into the crater, to get rid of his troubles."

"But look at that!" he went on in lighter tones. "That tree arched over the road just ahead—it has a lovely name, the Love Me Again tree. Do you see how the wind pushes the blossoms apart? And then how they lie close together once more? If you listen closely you will hear them whisper, 'Love me—love me again!' "

Bold and idle, a buzzard hung high overhead, stitched against the bright sky. Soon we could have looked almost at a level into his hungry eyes. The air had the sting of a New York fall.

"Angela will be feeling ashamed, of course," said Rodovaldes suddenly.

"Ashamed? Why?"

"Because she didn't come down to the hospital yesterday. It never occurred to me before: she'll think you must look on her as a coward. I wonder—I wonder if there isn't some way around that. . . . Would you mind very much if we pretended that I made a mistake in the date?"

"Of course not," I said.

He glanced at me apologetically. "I'm sorry to be such a nuisance about this, but as I told you, she's very sensitive. Once, after that experience in town, with the children hooting at her, she cried it must be some fault of hers, in some way she was to blame for how she looked. I told her that was nonsense, but I'm sure the idea's always been at the back of her mind. And now she'll feel she lacked the courage, lacked the faith, to help herself."

Hearing our car labouring up the mountain grade, Rodovaldes' housekeeper and other servants had assembled in front of the farmhouse to see who was coming, for this lonely road was seldom travelled. I looked around for the face that had been in my mind ever since Rodovaldes had first mentioned his Ugly Duchess.

"Where is the *señorita*?" Rodovaldes asked.

"The *señorita*?" the housekeeper repeated. "But she is in the city, *Señor*. She told us you expected her."

"In the city? When did she leave?"

"Yesterday morning, *Señor*."

He turned to me with a mirthless smile. "I see what must have happened. She went down there exactly as we had arranged but at the last moment couldn't get herself to go through with it. No doubt she's on her way back here now. Perhaps by the time we're finished with lunch——"

But half an hour, an hour passed by after lunch, and still no car had climbed the mountain road bringing the missing girl, and her brother was no longer able to disguise his uneasiness. "Do you mind waiting a little longer? No? That's very kind of you. . . . But there's no sense sitting here. Let me show you around the place."

We inspected it thoroughly; the silence and the tension grew. Where was she? What had happened to her?

"But I'm a poor sort of guide!" Rodovaldes exclaimed. "Here we have one of the greatest sights the whole country has to offer almost right at hand, and I've neglected to take you there! Can you spare another hour or two?"

I nodded, and we got back into his car and started up the road. It twisted and turned like a goat track, demanding all Rodovaldes' attention. Half a dozen times my heart was in my mouth as another dizzy precipice yawned before us, and by the time we stopped I felt worn out. The road by now had turned into only the roughest kind of trail and the car was perched there at a crazy angle; Rodovaldes pulled the hand brake back all the way and wedged two large rocks beneath the rear wheels. He gestured to the trail ahead.

"From here on I'm afraid we'll have to go on foot—but believe me, when we get there, the spectacle's worth it," he said, again with that artificial smile, and led the way, at a pace so brisk it was all I could do to keep up with him.

Greasy with rain, tattered grey wisps of clouds rushed past us. The climb seemed eternal. I was about to give up, exhausted, when Rodovaldes came to an abrupt halt, peering down at something in front of him, half eagerly, half fearfully. I clambered to his side.

There below us was spread out the crater of the volcano, old Irazu herself.

For half an hour we stared at that great rocky waste. Then my companion gave a sigh and the tension of his face somewhat relaxed. For there was nothing else there; Irazu had not had her taste of blood to-day.

Neither of us said anything, but each knew what the other was thinking: Angela the Ugly Duchess, sick of herself and of the world, had not come this way.

There was nothing to do except return to the city. Dusk was pooling in the streets when we arrived. I asked Rodovaldes to take me to the hospital, so that I could look in on the cases I had treated the day before. Then at last he came out with our unspoken secret:

"I've been very poor company for you, Doctor, but the truth is, I'm worried. The state of mind she must be in, I don't know what she might have done to herself." His eye fell on the entrance to the hospital chapel; it was almost exactly the same hour when I had seen him coming out of it yesterday. He had prayed for her then, so he had told me, and now he turned and went into the chapel, and I followed him.

It was very small, very quiet; the dim light was rich and deep as an old painting. Rodovaldes got to his knees and bowed his head. After a while he rose, and as he did so, another figure which had been kneeling in prayer, rose too. I saw her look at Rodovaldes.

"Tomas," she said.

In the dim, gracious light, her poor face was not so hopelessly ugly; for a moment, as her brother looked at her and realized that he had found his Ugly Duchess, it might almost have been said to be beautiful.

Later we heard the story. She had come to the city the day before, as they had told us at the farm, and had almost got to the hospital when, on the crowded street, the old panic of years ago seized her again, and she fled, searching for a place in which to hide.

There was a lodging house not far away; she took a room and locked herself in for the rest of the day and night, sleepless, eating and drinking nothing, cowering on the bed and weeping like the little girl who had been stoned by the mob.

And then, with the next day, towards sundown, a change had taken place in her spirit. She thought suddenly of the concern and anguish she must have been giving her brother.

Leaving the room, holding her head high, ignoring the curious stares and snickers of the outside world, she had gone to the hospital to find Tomas, and had stopped for a moment first in the chapel to pray.

Although, as I have said, you cannot build a new face, I saw that a good deal could be done for Angela. And after all hers was a face that had known beauty: the beauty of that moment when she saw who it was that was praying beside her, and knew for whom his prayers had been offered, as hers had been offered for him.

Perhaps her prayer expressed the surest of all paths to staying young: faith in yourself, faith in others, faith in God.

ISCHIA

The Young Hermit Who Discovered
"Another Room"

IN 1948 I HAD OCCASION TO GO TO ITALY; AND AFTER FINISH-
ing the task that had called me there, I spent several days in
wandering. From someone or other I heard about Ischia and
determined to visit it.

The island of Ischia grows like a black stone fist from the
floor of the Mediterranean where it shelves down to great
blue-purple depths beyond the Bay of Naples. If you approach
its southernmost point in the early-morning mists you will
think you have found another enchanted Avalon floating in the
sky, for the solid stone underpinning is veiled from sight and
you are aware only of castle towers and parapets, bathed pale
salmon pink by the dim sun.

But as the mists clear you see that it is not a fairy castle, it is
a town—a very tiny one, true, but complete with burghers'
houses and church and market place and guarding citadel high
overhead. A lovely place to live, surrounded by the blue of
sea and sky! Then, as your boat comes closer still, you feel the
coolness of the black rock, and the little town's astonishing
secret is revealed.

No curious faces peer down at you; the market place is
empty; only the gulls' mewing breaks the silence. High on its
rock, the town lies dreaming in the sunlight, and again you
think of a fairytale palace, held mute in some ageless spell.
The truth is, it is deserted, and has been for a hundred years or
more. Why?

The reason is not so dramatic as you might expect; after centuries of siege and counter-siege, when French, Italian and Spanish princes held the citadel turn and turn about, the end came in slow, quiet instalments. The people from the little town simply drifted to the mainland, until by 1790 less than a hundred were left there, where once there had been thousands. Soon these followed too, and the long silence began.

A great tunnel carved out of the rock brings you up to this ghost town. The sunlight fades behind, moisture glistens on the rough-chiselled walls, and the shades of the distant past seem to whisper around you, the Crusaders who paused here on their way to the Holy Land, the feudal lords, the Barbary corsairs, rough, clamorous, war-scarred men, gone now and long forgotten, except here in the gloom.

But now ahead, relieving it, there is a flicker of yellow light, and as you come around a curve of the tunnel you find a shrine to the Virgin, small, ancient, beautiful. In front of it the flame of a votive candle burns steadily, without dip or tremble in the unstirring air.

Puzzled, I turned to my guide.

"Who put the candle here, if the town is deserted?"

"Not entirely deserted, sir. One man stays here, winter and summer. You will see him soon."

We climbed on. The tunnel curved again, more sharply, and sunlight burst on us. Dazzled, I drew my breath and peered around and discovered that we were in the very heart of the town. There was the church, gaping roofless at the sky, though its deep stone flanks were sturdy as ever. A lizard scuttered over the dry, dusty pavement of the square and the gulls cried mournfully.

"Here, sir," said my guide, beckoning from a parapet. "Here is something interesting."

There was an appalling drop below where he stood, a sheer, smooth sweep of rock, hundreds of feet down to the sea. The boulders clustered at the base seemed no bigger than pebbles.

"Here, where I stand, was a favourite place in the old days," my guide continued. "It was here that they would bring traitors, criminals, captured enemies. They would bind them and place them here, so, and leave them to meditate on their sins for an hour or two and admire the view—magnificent, sir, is it not?—while the townfolk jeered at them and urged them to grow wings, for very soon they would be in sore need of them. At length the executioners would approach and everything would be very quiet, much as it is now. Then a push, a little push, and you would hear a scream in the air, falling, falling." He peered down at the dizzy drop. "It must have been a long death," he said reflectively.

Each moment I had been expecting to hear a voice hail us. "Where is the man you told me about?" I asked.

"The caretaker? In his room, I suppose, sir; it is about time for the midday meal."

"So he has a job, has he? Caretaker of the town?"

The guide shrugged. "We call him that, but what is there to look after? Stones, dust, empty houses. It's just the name he answers to. If he has any other, he's never told us."

"Where is his room?"

"In the bishop's palace. We can go there now, if you wish."

We crossed the square, threaded through a crooked alley, and entered the courtyard of the palace. The flight of steps leading to the splendid arched gateway were soft and warm with dust that deadened our footsteps. Yet from somewhere I heard a sound of alarm, a peculiar sound, wistful and arrogant. It brayed again; then I knew what it was. A goat.

And at that second the creature came bounding down the steps, a beautiful white-furred animal, daintily kept, her large liquid eyes peering at us with an almost human curiosity. She called once more, but now the sound was purely wistful. Poor thing, I thought, she must be very lonely, with a bishop's palace for her home!

127

She followed us like a pet dog, now and again uttering her wistful cry. Within the palace—but you were not really "within"; all the time the blue sky stared at you and the sun streamed through the gaps in the vaulted roof—one stately chamber led straight into another. In the fifteenth century, architects had yet to invent corridors to act as a buffer, a neutral zone, between rooms. If your sleeping chamber was the last of several, you had to walk through all the others to get to it.

But here there was no one's privacy to offend; where once the bishops of Ischia had prayed and slept, here came a guide and a tourist, the white nanny-goat bringing up the rear.

We reached the final room. It was perched like an eagle's nest above the island, and the view made my head swim. Rank upon rank, the dappled, sun-stained buildings fell away beneath, down to the bastion walls. Then your eye took the plunge to the carpet of the sea, stretching mile after mile, winking and shining, until it blended with the mists of the horizon. And there lay a dark blur, soft as smoke, which was Italy.

"Welcome," someone said.

The view had blinded me to everything else. In only that respect—the dimension given to it by its broad window—was the room large. Scarcely bigger than a monk's cell, it was furnished as plainly: a pallet on the floor, a jug of water and a basin, two or three boxes of food. And before one of them sat the room's tenant, inspecting us over his bread and cheese.

I had expected to find a swaybacked old fellow, full of bile and fleas; but the hermit of Ischia was not only young, he was impeccably clean. He had dark, pensive eyes and a full head of curly black hair. He wore a peasant's shirt and trousers and rough leather sandals.

"Help yourselves, please," he said politely, indicating the bread and cheese. But we had brought our own, with sausage and a flask of wine, and we urged him to share with us. After many protests he did, but only, I think, not to seem unappreciative.

He didn't seem curious at all about our presence, for he said nothing during the meal. When we were finished he filled the basin and with the same grave politeness offered it to us, and a scrap of towel. He tossed the water out of the window and it spread and shattered in the sunlight and seemed to fall a million miles, as slowly as a drifting bird. Then he filled the basin again and attended to himself, and sat back and regarded us calmly.

"Your view must make up for a good deal," I said.

"Make up?" he said. "For what?"

"Well, the solitude."

"Ah, yes, the solitude," he repeated, smiling. "Yes, it's true I was very much aware of it, when I first came to Ischia."

"When was that?" I asked.

"I haven't any calendar, but it must be seven or eight months, for she"—and he nodded to something behind me—"was very small then."

A silent presence had joined us. She had been content to sit in the doorway, inspecting the newcomers, but now she rose, arched her back lazily and promenaded across the room. She paused underneath the window, glanced over her shoulder as if to reassure herself that we were watching, then sprang up, so boldly that I thought she had misjudged the distance and would fall into the gulf of sky and sea. But of course she had not. Stretched at full length on the window ledge, with superb aplomb she began to wash her face.

"What a beautiful cat!"

"Isn't she?" the young man agreed. "She was only a kitten when I got her, barely weaned, so she knows nothing else but this island. I wonder sometimes if it does not seem remarkable to her that, so far as she can see, she is the only cat in the whole wide world!"

E

"Do you mind if I ask you why you took up this solitary life?"

"I suppose I'm a mysterious figure," he replied, smiling again, "but I'm afraid there's nothing mysterious about the whole thing, really. No broken love affair, no vendetta, nothing like that. Simply boredom."

"It seems to me you couldn't have had much cause to complain of that," I said.

"No?"

"You're a good-looking young man. Surely you must have lots of friends."

He considered me for a few minutes. I sensed that now one of two things would happen: courteously but firmly he would bring our interview to an end by refusing to say another word about himself, or he would come out with the whole story. There was no way to influence his decision; I could only hope that he had reached the point in his self-imposed exile where he would feel the need to explain his reasons for it.

I saw the focus of his eyes shift from the present to the past and knew he had decided to talk.

"Yes, I had lots of friends," he said. "In that respect I was what is thought of as fortunate. I suppose you would say in every respect. My parents were indulgent and seldom refused me anything I asked for, and when it came time to think of a job I just about had my choice. Whatever I chose, I would be assured through my father's influence of stepping into some easy berth where the only essential would be to cut a good figure. An excellent marriage had been arranged for me, the girl was attractive, her family was wealthy, I was even a little bit in love with her. There seemed to be nothing in my life or in my prospects for the future—except that I was bored to death.

"I discovered this one evening when I was dressing to go to a party. A lot of pretty girls who offered interesting possibilities would be there, and I knew exactly how I proposed to take advantage of them. I kept a boat down in the harbour and later on I would suggest going out for a moonlight sail—on this hot summer night, the invitation would be irresistible.

"I was brushing my hair, I remember, when suddenly, I couldn't understand why, everything seemed flat. Not only the evening ahead; my whole life. Then a stupid, incongruous thing happened. I sneezed. This cheered me up. I had a cold or something or other coming on; obviously this flatness of spirit was simply one of the symptoms. I thought with relief that now I could excuse myself from the party and take some aspirin and go to bed, so as to get over the cold or whatever it was as soon as possible and return to my normal self.

"Then I thought, no, I'll be damned if I will. I'd taken a lot of trouble fixing up the boat, stocking the galley with champagne and caviar and lobster salad and God knows what else, and it seemed a shame to waste it. At least I should give it a whirl. After a few drinks I was bound to feel better. So I told myself.

"The party was a very gala affair and the prettiest girl there appeared to take a special interest in me. Everything went according to plan. When I proposed going down for a sail, she agreed right away; and at around two in the morning, there we were gliding over the Bay of Naples in the moonlight. I had the tiller under one arm and the other around the girl, who was extremely affectionate. With the moonlight and the soft breeze and the rustle of the water along the hull, what more could you ask for?"

He was silent for a few minutes. On the window ledge, the cat finished washing her face and gazed around through half-lidded eyes. Her lazy stare came to rest on her master. She seemed to sense that his attention was not on her but on that scene in the past, for she uttered a small, querulous sound, sprang down from her perch, marched over to him and rubbed her body against his arm.

He stroked her absently. "And yet," he resumed, "there it

was again, as suddenly as before and, God knows, even more inexplicable. What the devil was happening to me? I should be attending to my knitting, getting on with the proper business of the evening. But instead, I was overwhelmed by this horrible bleakness of spirit that made everything stupid and dreary.

"The girl was aware of the change in me, of course, if only in the slackened pressure of my arm around her; and she leaned closer. I did my best to respond but it was no use.

"She sat up and tidied her hair. 'It must be getting terribly late,' she said. 'Are we going anywhere in particular?'

"An absolutely mad thing came into my mind. 'Yes,' I said, 'to Ischia.'

"She stared at me. 'Ischia!' she cried. 'That gloomy old place? You must be crazy!'

"Privately, I was ready to agree with her.

" 'Besides,' she went on, 'even if I wanted to go, it's much too far. We'd never be able to make the trip over and back tonight, and there are loads of things I have to do to-morrow. In fact,' she added coolly, 'if you don't mind, I think we'd better be turning back now.'

" 'Just as you say,' I agreed, and swung the tiller over.

"Nothing more was said until I saw her to her door and wished her good night. She gave me a curious look as we parted. I couldn't blame her. Here was a young man who up to a certain point had behaved normally and satisfactorily, with the proper ardour, the proper caresses. Then, almost at the second when she was ready to indicate that she would have no objection to letting the tiller of the boat take care of itself for a spell if the pilot wished to concern himself with other matters—poof! for no reason that she could see, he collapsed like a deflated balloon. And then, on top of everything, to tell her that they were bound for Ischia, at that hour! Why Ischia, of all places?

"The next day, I asked myself the same question. Why

Ischia, of all places? I hadn't thought of the deserted town at the tip of the island since the time many years before when my father had taken me there. Whatever had caused it to pop back into my head?

"I decided that it had occurred to me at random as something that would convince the girl it was time to go home.

"But in the days that followed I couldn't get the place out of my mind. And so one week-end I provisioned the boat and set out to have another look at the old town."

Pausing, he gazed out of the window at sea and sky, glittering in the full tide of noonday sun. The cat had fallen asleep; outside the door, the nanny-goat slumbered too. My guide's head drooped a little. The heat and the absolute silence—for at this height the sound of the water on the rocks below did not reach us, and the sky was empty of the mewing gulls—were almost irresistible.

The quiet voice resumed its story.

"If you approach Ischia in the morning, as you must have, you know how beautiful it is. I made the boat fast and jumped ashore, climbed up through the tunnel, and came out into the square below. And that was when I realized that the dead, dull weight that had been oppressing me was gone.

"I could have dropped to my knees and given thanks. Why the island should have that effect on me I didn't know; but there it was, and with light heart I set out to explore the deserted town.

"Though by nightfall I was physically tired, my spirits were still high. I had intended to sleep on the boat but such was the spell of the island that I decided instead to spend the night on shore. I found this room and for hours sat staring out of the window. The view changed as the night deepened and the moon rose. Ischia looks quite different at night; the towers and the walls and the parapets of the old town are magnified and distorted into grotesque patterns, like a painting by El Greco—grotesque at first, strange and cruel; but then, just as with the painting, as your eye grows accustomed to it the inner beauty unfolds like a flower and eclipses even that of the day. Though the day is good too.

"I was so absorbed by this scene that I can't remember sleeping at all the first night. Then towards dawn an extraordinary thing happened. You will say it was a dream, but it was not. Suddenly I could see myself as you see me now; that is to say, I was no longer I, I could inspect myself from the outside, through other eyes. And more remarkable still, I was given the power to understand this man I stared at so curiously and I was able to answer the questions that had been puzzling me. I knew why I had felt the terrible desolation of spirit; I knew why I had been seized with the impulse to come to Ischia.

"I had felt bored to death. Of course. That boredom had come from sheer surfeit, from yielding to every appetite until none was left. Where there is no interest or eagerness for anything, that is death, death in youth, death in the midst of life.

"Then I had remembered a happy day when I was a boy, the day my father had taken me on an excursion to this old island. I remembered the sparkling eyes of a boy, the fast-beating heart, the keen anxiety to see and understand everything of the marvellous world that lay around him. How happy I had been then, how young, how very much alive! And so, reaching out for that lost youth and happiness, I had come back here as a man.

"That first day, I had seemed to be the adventuring boy again, which was why my spirits had lifted the moment I had set foot on the island. But the illusion would not last; it was bound to pall soon; and then what? Was there nothing for it then but to return to that familiar world of surfeit, where everything was mine for the asking and nothing was worth asking for?

"I realized that the two extremes were there before me: the world of the mainland, the city, the crowds, the frantic gaiety piled on top of the frantic work to scratch your way ahead of the other fellow: and here, Ischia, the old deserted town. Here, if I was going to find pleasure and interest in life, I would have to find it in myself. And if I could do that, then I would be proof against the boredom and the torments and the surfeits and the tension of that other world.

"Did I have the strength to test that idea? I resolved to try. I returned home and said that I was leaving on a trip that would keep me away for perhaps a year. Then I came here.

"But now my time, I feel, is almost up—eight months, nine months—not much longer now. I am not anxious to go back but I am ready for it."

He paused, and his eyes slowly came back to the present. "The Muslims, you know," he observed, "hold that a man should fast—that is to say, should restrict himself severely in every aspect of his life—for a month every year, not to the detriment of his health, but to discipline the body, to purify the flesh and the spirit. I think of these past eight or nine months in that way—a fast. This has been none too long a time to give to it, considering how many years I had squandered away heedlessly, never stopping to regard myself, to find that interior life that waits in everyone if he will only search for it."

One thing seemed obvious enough, I thought as the young man paused again. "It isn't everyone who can afford to come to an Ischia for eight or nine months."

"That is true," he agreed tranquilly. "But my case was extreme. I think I shall never need Ischia again, because of what she has taught me. That is, that there can be an Ischia everywhere: another room, a quiet room, the room next door: a place to retreat to, to be alone in, for the discovery of yourself."

HOSPITAL ROOM

The Visitor from Yesterday

A COSMOPOLITAN GROUP OF PASSENGERS WAITED AT THE Naples airport for the London plane. I felt I could pretty well pick out my countrymen, and the English, and the Italians; and of course the two Hindu women in their beautiful saris were immediately identifiable.

But the small stocky man over there, in the beige-coloured suit and silk shirt and high, stiff white collar, what was he? He looked so very neat and clean and also, I saw now, so old-fashioned. His felt hat was of the style you saw in the beginning years of the century (it almost seemed to be supported by his protruding ears), and his shoes were the final touch: high, pale brown shoes, with sharp tips, and buttoned right up the sides.

As I studied the short, stocky man, with his dark eyes and his black hair and his broad, rather pale face with the beaked nose, I began to think I had met him before; but search though I would through my memory I couldn't pin down the time and place. By and by the plane trundled up and we got on board.

My "mysterious traveller" and I found ourselves directly across the aisle from each other. So it was impossible for me not to see how he dealt with his lunch when it was delivered to us. He put the knife and fork supplied by the airline to one side and from his waistcoat pocket drew out a small brown object that looked as if it contained eye-glasses. But no; it yielded instead a pearl-handled knife with folding blade and an equally collapsible fork.

137

Then my mysterious traveller fell to, with good appetite and irreproachable demeanour. Finished with the main course, he washed his personal knife and fork in the finger-bowl, put the fork away in its case, and with the knife carved up an apple as delicately and precisely as a master surgeon. The apple done with, he washed the knife again, folded it and put it to rest with the fork; put the case back in his pocket and sipped some cognac with the air of a man who knows what he likes.

In England, I had an engagement to keep at the Nuffield Department of Plastic Surgery at Oxford, headed by my friend Professor Pomfrit Kilner. My lecture went off in due course and I continued on to New York.

A backlog of work had piled up at the office and after a week of crowded days I felt tired and out of sorts. Sitting down with a cigar that somehow had no taste, I glanced at the picture of my father on the side table and fell to thinking again of the tragedy that had ended his life.

At that time Dad was a broad-shouldered man in his middle fifties, a commanding, erect person, his dark hair unstreaked by so much as a thread of grey, his eyes keen and direct as a youth's. So long as I could remember he had worn a full, sweeping moustache, and in his rare moments of anger this would seem to bunch together and rise up a little on his face, an effect caused by the way Dad would purse his lips in a thin straight line.

It was a constant battle for him to control that temper of his; none of his children ever saw it unleashed. His hand—and a hefty one it was—would never strike anyone, even when something particularly stupid happened in his workrooms (he was a fabric designer). For once, years before, in a moment of passion caused by an argument over who had been responsible for sickness in the family, he struck my mother. For that he never forgave himself; he would never again strike any living thing.

Dad was the neighbourhood's arbitrator, along with that other judge, philosopher and story-teller, Mr. Cremona, the barber. To settle family arguments or commercial disputes helped him to forget his rheumatism, Dad maintained. Ah, that rheumatism! It would be heralded in the early morning by little sighs and mutterings coming from Dad's room, and though these should have caused us all to feel properly sympathetic and sorry for him, alas, they did not; instead, no matter how sombre the day, we immediately cheered up and awaited coming events with eager anticipation. For an onslaught of Dad's rheumatism meant that Mr. Cremona would be called in with his magic black bag.

And in a little while there he would be, this roly-poly butterball of a man, even more fully mustachioed than Dad, to compensate, we imagined, for the bald head above. He would inspect Dad, give him a small pat, and open the black bag. Out would come the first of his marvels: some cotton, then a wooden probe, then a bottle of alcohol. He would wind the cotton with swift, expert fingers around the probe, dip it in alcohol, and put a match to it. Then, while holding the flaming taper in his left hand, he would dive his right into the black bag and bring out a handful of small glass cups. Swiftly the burning cotton would be passed under the cups, to suck out the air, and then one by one they would be clapped on to Dad's bare back. Within a few minutes he would look knobby, horned, a kind of human dragon with a gnarled skin of glass bumps.

This was the process of "cupping," a famous old-world remedy. The theory was that the vacuum under the glass cups brought the blood to the surface and thus by counter-irritation relieved your rheumatics. And I feel sure it did. At least it could do no harm, and always, after Mr. Cremona's visit and the laying-on of the cups, Dad professed himself to be enormously improved.

My father was an extremely tidy man, very fussy about

every detail of his appearance, clothes, shoes, hair, fingernails. To see him get ready in the morning for the street and the workroom was an impressive experience.

But one day each year all this was forgotten. On that day, Dad wouldn't shave, his moustache would go untrimmed, his hair unbrushed. All day he would stay cloistered in his room; none would be permitted to enter or even to address so much as a word to him. Towards sundown he would come out. But how changed!

No longer the fashion plate; gone, the silk shirt, the high starched collar, the rich tie with its fine pattern, the beautifully cut suit, the cuff-links, the burnished shoes, winking like jewels. In their place he wore an old shabby jacket and frayed trousers made of cheap cloth, and boots warped at the seams, and a peculiar greenish hat, so much fingered it was beginning to take on the shine of leather.

For these were the clothes he had worn when arriving as an immigrant from Austria, years before. He had kept them carefully, and this day each year he put them on again, to remember, and to be as humble as he had been then; and, so dressed, once more the poor immigrant, he would go to the Temple to give thanks, for his family, for his happiness, for everything he had found in America.

In other ways too he gave thanks for his good fortune. One day Tony, a boy down the block, fell afoul of the toughest youth in the neighbourhood. This was Whitey, much feared by all. Whitey vowed solemnly that he would teach Tony his place by branding him with "Whitey's sign," a knife slash across the left cheek. Dad learned of this as he was sitting on a pier looking over the East River, enjoying the air and the cries of the gulls and the ever-changing river parade of boats small and large; for here came Tony panting towards him, young face livid with fear.

"What's the trouble?" Dad asked.

"Whitey!" Tony gasped, and poured out the story, clutching his cheek as if it had been cut already. "He's back there, coming for me now!"

"Get down there," Dad said, pointing to some wooden steps leading under the pier; and Tony did as he said.

Presently Dad saw Whitey peering around at the end of the pier and called to him. When the boy came over Dad said: "There's something I thought you'd like to know. I've got a lot of hope for young Tony Finettra—you know him, don't you?"

Whitey admitted he did.

"I think he'll make a fine designer—fabric-designer—so I'm going to give him some lessons in my shop. My own boy just doesn't lean that way. You ought to come around some time, Whitey; might be something you'd be interested in." Dad got up. "Of course," he concluded in a casual tone, "if anything happened to Tony, considering the hopes I have for him, I'd be very—very—un*happy*." And he gave Whitey a friendly slap on the back.

Of course, with those big shoulders of his, Dad often underestimated his own strength, and this friendly slap almost sent Whitey into the East River. At any rate, there was no more trouble.

No, I did not lean that way; my leaning was towards medicine. My first day as an interne was to be a great one for the family; Dad had arranged to come up to see me at the hospital in my brand-new white jacket and trousers, then escort me home in triumph for dinner, and bring me back to the hospital again.

But he never saw me in the interne's proud uniform. He was too impatient and excited to go on working in the shop that afternoon, so finally he gave up and started to walk to the hospital, pausing every few steps to announce to friends and neighbours where he was going and why. He got to Second Avenue, and there a truck lunged out of control and climbed up on the sidewalk and killed him.

Well, I had much to remember, much to thank him for, and once in a while, as I thought about him, he seemed to come very close to me, almost close enough to touch, to hear his voice again.

I had a final appointment for the day and went in to keep it. Nothing could have been better calculated to wrench me out of my reverie about Dad than the sight of the man who had come to see me. There he stood, my "mysterious traveller," the stocky, neat gentleman with the high button shoes who had been on the plane with me from Naples to London.

"You are astonished, Doctor?" he said, seeing the expression on my face.

I admitted it.

"Not so strange as you may think," he told me. "I asked who you were when you left the plane in London and they told me something about you. Something else I confess. I felt, I do not know how to say it without perhaps seeming a little foolish, but—I felt, Doctor, a certain sympathy between us, if you will excuse me, though we spoke nothing to each other. Well, now, you see these?"—and he indicated the out-jutting ears—"and this?"—and here he gave a light dab to the great humped beak on his nose—"these I have always been self-conscious about, in my business, and now since I have some extra time, if it does not seem, what do you say, conceited and foolish to you—I would like you to make them look better, if you can."

"I don't think it's foolish of you," I said.

"Then you can do it?"

"Yes, certainly."

"Ah, good. You can do it soon, Doctor?"

He entered the hospital the next evening and the following morning was brought into the operating room. All went smoothly and we were finished soon. That evening I stopped in to visit him. Face swathed in bandages, he told me he felt in excellent spirits and was looking forward keenly to the result. I found it extremely pleasant to talk to him and stopped by at least twice a day during the next week, until the great day came, and we took off the last bandages.

For the second time he saw an expression of vast astonishment come over my face.

"Is something wrong, Doctor?"

I reached for the hand mirror. "No, no. See for yourself."

He inspected the new nose, the new ears—and, too, the moustache he had grown during his convalescence, to save as much trouble as possible with shaving.

"Good," he exclaimed. "Good, good!" And then regarded me. "But the way you looked——"

There was no need, really, to ask him the questions that came thronging into my head, for somehow I knew what the answers would be; yet I did.

"You are from Austria, aren't you, I think you told me?"

"Yes," he said. "Vienna."

"May I know what your business is there?"

"I work with fabrics," he answered. "I am a designer. Why?"

"It's an odd coincidence," I said. "I knew a fabric-designer once. He came from Austria too."

I didn't go beyond that; it would have passed his belief, as it passed mine. For with the moustache and the change in the nose, there he was, looking at me again—my father, almost as I had seen him last, the morning of the day he had started up Second Avenue to visit me at the hospital.

Suddenly, the past had become the present. I felt myself to be a young man of twenty-four again, but with one great difference. I realized now, as I had never fully realized then, how much I owed that kindly, strong man. He had always been a *young* father to me, not the grim, remote stranger I saw in other families; and I knew how he had kept himself young. It was quite simple, really—by offering his friendship and help and advice to all the youth of our neighbourhood.

143

SAN MIGUEL

Hercules and the Island That Let Off Steam

THE GREAT AIRLINER LIFTED UP SMOOTHLY FROM IDLEWILD
and soon was far out over the dark Atlantic, headed for
the Azores. Almost within minutes of our departure my
travelling companion settled back in his chair, closed his eyes
and was asleep. As I glanced at him I chuckled to myself. How
much at ease you are, my dear Josué, I thought, and how very
different your behaviour was when we first met, just about
ten years ago!

At that time, Josué and I had been travelling companions on
another plane, an old, battered, wing-weary DC 3. But in war-
time we had been lucky to get any kind of air passage and had
no complaints. This venerable craft was bound for Rio, where
I was to give a series of lectures at the invitation of a former
pupil of mine, Dr. Luthero Vargas.

At the moment when I first became sharply aware of the
man in the seat next to me, we were some five thousand feet
above the Amazon jungle. He was a good-looking, well-
dressed young fellow and previously had given me no cause
for concern. But now he began to fidget. It was soon more
than fidgeting, it was a definite squirming. At last I couldn't
stand his nervousness any longer.

"Excuse me," I said, "is there anything I can do?"

He looked at me with rolling eyes. "No, nothing, thank
you."

"Are you sure? I'm a doctor."

145

"It's not a doctor we need," he said with great agitation, "it's a magician."

"A magician? What for?"

"Do you mean to say you can't hear it?"

I listened. I could hear nothing except the engine roar.

"Well?" he said impatiently.

"I don't notice anything," I said. "Just the racket of the engines."

"But of course!" he cried. "That's it! Hear the *rhythm*."

And now, sure enough, I was aware of a change in that steady beat: a cough, a stammer; and looking out of my window I could have sworn I saw a distinct slowing down of the port engine's blades. But then, a DC 3 could maintain flight on one of its two engines, or so I had always understood, and I mentioned this to my companion.

"Not this one," he informed me. "We're so much overloaded I was amazed when we managed to get off the ground. No, there's nothing else for it, we're in for an emergency landing. They'll be making the announcement any second now."

I knew what an emergency landing in the green tangle of the Amazon jungle meant. It would be better to come down at sea; for this green surf beneath us would bury you under its matted vines and boughs; no raft would float on it.

The door to the pilots' compartment now opened and the steward appeared. "It is necessary to make an unscheduled landing," he said with a graveyard jauntiness. "Please adjust your seat belts, and please—no smoking."

"An unscheduled landing where?" someone asked.

"At Bereiras, madam, just ahead."

"Certainly it's just ahead," said my companion gloomily. "so is Rio. The question is, how to get there?"

"Isn't there any chance?"

"With the greatest good luck in the world, a slight one."

I closed my eyes and tried to resign myself. After an age—fifteen minutes, I suppose—there was a bang and a bump, and opening my eyes I saw the good earth rolling by outside the window—the emergency landing field hacked out of the jungle at Bereiras.

"We thank thee, merciful Mother of God!" cried my companion, crossing himself rapidly. "And believe me," he added, in a different tone but just as emphatically, "after this, I'll never fly again."

Well, so he had said, and I'd believed him then. But of course he did fly again, many, many times. His business brought him frequently to New York and he always stopped in to see me, as I did to see him when I was in Rio. And it was one of these visits that had brought about our present trip.

Josué was not a native of Brazil but of that first Portuguese stepping stone on the long sea route to Brazil, the Azores. He and his sister had grown up on the tiny island of San Miguel. Then Josué had gone on to Rio and into business as a coffee broker and established himself and a fine young family. Back at home, his sister had married too, and once every two years or so it was possible for Josué to get over to see her and her husband and their first baby.

This was a charming child named Rose. Josué's last visit had coincided with her second birthday. But there was not the merrymaking he would have expected; and when he saw Rose, he understood why.

"When did this happen?" he asked.

"At first we thought it was nothing," his sister answered. "We thought it would go away by itself. But, as you see——"

The ugly lump over the little girl's left eye had grown to about the size of a walnut. So that was the mission that was bringing us to San Miguel now, to see what could be done. It would all depend on how far the growth had advanced; if it had gone beyond a certain point it might be impossible to operate without irreparable damage.

At the airport at Santa Maria we had a cup of coffee and a bite to eat and then boarded the inter-island plane for San

Miguel. Josué's family and friends had gathered to meet us, a handsome group of people, with one exception, his uncle. He cut a pathetic figure, this weedy little fellow with the drooping moustache. He murmured his name timidly as I shook his hand, and of all the names in the world to choose from, his parents had baptized him "Hercules." I wondered why on earth he hadn't changed it; for on hearing that bold name for the first time and seeing the frail figure that bore it, it was difficult to keep back a smile.

And here was Rose, all in white, with a hat just a bit too large for her, so that you thought of a shy little pixie hiding within a shell. Rose was the right name for her, in contrast to poor Milquetoast—the right name for her, that is, if you excepted one side of her face. For her left eye could no longer be seen; the eyelids were almost completely shut, and near the outer aspect of the eyebrow was the ugly mass that was responsible.

But, on first examination at least, an operation to remove the growth seemed perfectly possible. So I informed the family, and the atmosphere cheered up. We got into the waiting cars and began the drive to their home.

That was a fascinating journey. It carried us through the fertile hills of San Miguel, and all the riches of the bountiful earth lay around us. Blue hydrangeas were massed along the roadside, like gigantic leis; and up above on the hill slopes houses of a hundred different shades of colour seemed to be so many different flowers themselves. The broad white wings of windmills turned lazily in the warm breeze, cattle of an extraordinary plumpness grazed in the fields; and here was a whole flashing acre of glass, the hothouses where the succulent pineapples of San Miguel were forced to extra plumpness and sweetness.

Then came a field of tea bushes, and then of tobacco plants; and now and again we passed drowsy oxen pulling the groaning thick-wheeled carts to market. In the valleys beneath the vine-wreathed bridges grew New Zealand ferns, and Japanese camellias, and Scandinavian abies. All this and more was explained to me by my hosts, while Rose—worn out with the trip and the excitement—slept in her mother's arms.

So we came to our destination, the town of Ponta Delgada. Here the scene was busier. For the first time I saw carts drawn by sheep, and there were so many dogs trotting along in a businesslike way with packages in their mouths that I asked what they were doing.

"Messenger dogs," I was told. "It's almost noon and they're bringing their masters' lunch from home."

The next morning further examination confirmed my first opinion: that the growth over Rose's eye had not gone too far to forbid surgery. She was anæsthetized—she went under perfectly willingly, for her mother's hand held her own, and small Uncle Hercules was there too.

I cut through the skin near the left eyebrow, undermined the tissue quite extensively; and then, lifting the edges of the skin with delicate hooks, I shelled out the encapsulated growth that had burrowed deep down to the skull. Finally I approximated the edges of the wound with separate sutures of five-zero black silk, as fine as human hair, and dressed the area. And then Rose was wheeled from the operating room still asleep and put back to bed.

Two hours later she woke up. There was her mother, and there was Hercules, and her father too.

"Well, darling?" her mother asked. "Do you know what happened?"

Rose smiled sleepily. "Yes," she said in a tranquil voice. "I went away—and then I came back again." She felt the bandages around her head and looked puzzled.

"Something else went away too," Hercules informed her. "The lump over your eye. But it *won't* be back."

Well, it turned out I was wrong about Hercules: that preposterous name wasn't preposterous at all. I had ten days to wait before the last bandages over Rose's eye could be removed, and in those days he was my guide on many trips around the island. High in the mountains, he showed me San Miguel's two magic lakes, one green, the other blue, and told me their legend. In the old days, a humble shepherd had longed in vain for the king's lovely daughter; but, seeing him once tending his sheep, she fell in love with him. When the king learned her secret, he had her locked in the highest tower of the castle, and here the sad lady pined away—whereupon the shepherd boy promptly died too.

"And these, the waters of the two lakes," Hercules concluded, "are supposed to be the tears of those two who died for love."

Hercules himself, I thought, might one day be a legend in San Miguel. For the really remarkable thing about these sight-seeing trips was the number of people who clustered around us wherever we went. I couldn't make out what was going on, just a great amount of talk; Hercules always seemed to have the last word, and there was always quite a demonstration when we left. Finally I asked Josué what was behind all this.

"Ah, that Hercules," he said. "For a little fellow, he has a big, big brain. Anything goes wrong, people ask him what to do, and he settles things for them. If you want to know the truth, Max, *I* wasn't the one who thought of asking you here when they showed me the lump over Rose's eye, it was old Hercules who suggested it. He'd heard me talk about you and he said, 'Isn't that the kind of work the doctor does?' And do you know I'd never thought of it at all?"

One morning, for the *pièce de résistance*, Hercules showed me the grandest sight the Azores have to offer. Buried in the green, peaceful island was a valley of steam. These were the famous Furnas geysers, the *caldeiras*.

"There is a lesson here, when one thinks about it," Hercules remarked. "We are very lucky on San Miguel to have such rich soil and such good air to breathe. Much of the reason for it is in this valley. Don't you think, Doctor, that a man too is something of an island?"

He expanded then on what he meant, and I left the valley of the geysers thinking that his words were not so fanciful as they had seemed to me at first; no, I thought they made good sense. But then, by this time I realized that everything Hercules did or said made good sense.

On the tenth day I removed the last dressing, and there was Rose as she was meant to be: her face unmarred, and able to look at the world out of two eyes once more.

We had a party that night, and an excellent party it was. There were many speeches and much wine. The wine of San Miguel seemed to me as benign as the air of San Miguel, as innocent and artless as its people. I drank a good deal of it, deeply convinced of its innocence, its wholesome character; and suddenly I found myself on my feet and making a speech, though I had had no previous intention of doing so. A good deal that I said has escaped my memory, but I do remember one passage. It was what Hercules had told me.

"Ladies and gentlemen," I said, "others may search far and wide for the secret of your beautiful island, why the air is so pure and the earth so bountiful and life so good, but I know the reason—there is no tension here. And why is that? Because in your wonderful Furnas valley, the geysers let it all out! And yes, men are like islands, as my friend Hercules said. So if they'd only let off steam, as your island does, instead of bottling it up inside, it would help them to stay young and productive, just like your wonderful island."

How Molly Got Her Hat and
Mr. Hilden Became an Umpire

M Y VISITOR, A LADY IN HER THIRTIES, WAS IN SUCH A CON-
dition of internal pressure that she reminded me of a
kettle just coming to the boil. She had been waiting for half
an hour or so, rehearsing, I am sure, what she intended to say,
but now that we were face to face her emotions overcame her
and she got badly mixed up.

"Doctor," she began, swallowing and turning an even
brighter pink, "don't do it—don't do it, I beg of you, that is
all I have to ask: *Don't!*"

"Don't do what?" I said. But I might have saved my
breath.

"It's second childhood, Doctor," she steamed on, "that's
what it is, neither more nor less. I don't like to say such things,
but why fool yourself, when it's as plain as the nose on your
face? But what can I do? I can't have her committed, God
forbid I should even think of it, my own mother, and it's no
use talking to her, because she simply refuses to listen to
reason. I can say it until I am black and blue in the face,
'Mother, I will not permit it'—so why be barking up an
empty tree or locking the stable when the horse is gone, my
own mother I can't boss around, can I? So you understand,
Doctor, at last I saw there was only one thing to do. The
doctor, I said to myself, *he'll* be reasonable, so go to him! So,"
she concluded, waving her hands in a final burst of enlighten-
ment, "now you understand why I'm here!"

While she sat there puffing, I said, "No, I'm sorry, but I don't understand. Why *are* you here?"

"But I've just told you!"

"Suppose you start at the very beginning," I suggested. "What is it you don't want me to do?"

"Why," she said, puzzled that I should be so dense, "fix my mother's face, of course!"

"What's wrong with your mother's face?"

"Nothing, Doctor, absolutely nothing! That's what's so terrible, you understand? It's just the sort of face she should have for a woman of her age, sixty-two her last birthday. If she should be in an accident or something like that, God forbid, then naturally I'd make allowances. It's better to come here than to have people staring and whispering about you; but when there is nothing wrong, absolutely nothing, when it looks as nature intended, then there is only one answer, she is in her second childhood."

"Well," I said, "maybe you're right."

"I knew you'd agree! So you won't do it?"

"Perhaps I'd better not decide until I see your mother. But why are you so sure she's coming to see me?"

"You have an appointment with her this Wednesday, Doctor!"

"I have?"

Obviously this is a man who doesn't know his business; I could see that conviction written all over her.

"But of course, Doctor! With Mrs. Molly Arberman! Look in your appointment book and you'll see. I heard her make the appointment myself over the phone, calling your office and fixing the time and everything with your secretary, and then when I asked her what was wrong, she was going to a doctor's office, she looked at me as bold as brass and came right out with it, not ashamed or anything as anyone in his right mind would be at sixty-two years of age, when I said, 'What's it for, Mother? You're sick, you're calling the doctor?'

" 'Why no, Ruthie,' she said with a chuckle, laughing, Doctor, can you imagine? 'not sick like you think, Ruthie, but just sick of my *face*. I'm going to the doctor to talk about having it *lifted*!' "

At last the light came breaking through. "Ah!" I said. "So your mother wants to have her *face* lifted!"

"But of course!" Miss Ruth Arberman exclaimed. "Why, Doctor, what in the world do you think we've been talking about?"

And then she ran out of steam. She just sat heaving in her chair, pink and exhausted. I got her a glass of water and by and by, after she had finished it and looked less pink, I said:

"Now, Miss Arberman, something must have started all this, so won't you tell me what it was?"

She considered. When not steaming she was a nice-enough-looking woman but you could see she was accustomed to have everything in its proper place, just so.

"What started it?" she repeated. "Well, Doctor, now you ask, I guess it must have been Mr. Hilden's dog."

"Mr. Hilden's dog determined your mother to have her face lifted?"

She smiled. "That sounds foolish, doesn't it? But that was only in a manner of speaking. Mr. Hilden, you see, bought this dog four or five months ago, and—— But first I must tell you something about Mr. Hilden."

What follows, then (with the addition of later information), is what I learned about Mr. Hilden, Mr. Hilden's dog, and why Mrs. Molly Arberman had decided to have her face lifted.

Mr. Hilden, Mr. Maurice Hilden, had been following a set routine for almost three years, ever since the death of his beloved wife, Judith. At that time he had given up the apartment, no longer able to face the dear familiar rooms, now so silent, and had moved to a small hotel just off Jerome Avenue in the Bronx. Here Mr. Hilden would get up every morning

at six—he always had been an early riser—have his cup of coffee
and piece of Danish at the lunch-room down the block, buy
the *News* and his morning cigar and walk slowly down to the
little neighbourhood park, where he would sit on his favourite
bench, read his paper and smoke his cigar. He was generally
there first; by nine o'clock all the benches would be pretty
well filled, with gentlemen much of Mr. Hilden's age and circumstances, some of them widowers too.

There was a scattering of ladies but very little mixing between the sexes took place; the gentlemen were content to sit
and doze, the ladies to gossip. Frankly, Mr. Hilden thought
the women were a sad-looking bunch, fat old hens and lean
old biddies, cackling and gabbing, sitting in the sun and waiting for the time when the undertaker's wagon would come
along. But of course, he admitted, what else were you going
to do?

At twelve o'clock, Mr. Hilden would have his lunch, usually
at the Automat, and then repair to the hotel for a nap. Later
in the afternoon he did more sitting on the park bench, and
at five o'clock returned to the hotel to freshen up for dinner.
Mr. Hilden had always taken pride in presenting a neat appearance; Judith had said about him that he was "fastidious"—the
affectionate way she had said this had always given Mr. Hilden
a glow.

To tell the truth there had been a temptation to let things
slide after Judith's death, not change his shirt every day, not
keep his shoes shined, and skip shaving every morning; but
then Mr. Hilden had reflected that Judith would not like it,
and so before dinner he freshened up as always. God knows
no one in the restaurant where he had dinner gave a hoot
whether he was freshened up or not, nor at the movie afterward—Mr. Hilden was a devoted movie fan, particularly fond
of what he called sporting pictures, boxing, football, baseball
—baseball most of all.

However, you could not go to the movies every night,

there simply are not enough movies made, and so at least three nights a week Mr. Hilden found himself back in the park on the same bench or on cold nights back in his room listening to the radio.

On April 16, a beautiful spring day, Mr. Hilden celebrated his sixty-eighth birthday. He celebrated it by rising at six in the morning, having breakfast at the lunchroom down the block, buying the *News* and a cigar, and sitting on his favourite bench in the park. Well, there was nothing else to do. He and Judith had not been blessed with children and after her death he had gradually drifted away from their friends, because seeing them was almost like being back in the old apartment—he would be reminded of her so painfully the tears would come to his eyes. So there was no one to celebrate the sixty-eighth birthday with. Not that it mattered. Mr. Hilden wouldn't have paid any attention to his birthday at all if it had not meant that he was just that much closer to the end of the road he longed to reach.

On his way back to the park bench after lunch, an extraordinary event occurred.

Mr. Hilden became the owner of a dog.

He had no intention of becoming the owner of a dog; the ownership sort of crept up on him. Standing on the street corner was a thin, seedy-looking man, holding in his hands an even seedier-looking hat, and inside this hat was an animal that would have taxed the powers of description of a Shakespeare. It was a puppy, but such an absolutely absurd puppy that its ancestors for generations back must have been extremely promiscuous. Certainly there was a good dose of dachshund there, and a sprinkling of sheep dog, and here was a glimpse of airedale, and a whiff, maybe more, of some kind of bulldog.

Mr. Hilden could not help it; he paused and stared at this ludicrous animal and had a good laugh.

"You like heem?" the seedy-looking man said eagerly.

"Wan dollar, plizz." And before Mr. Hilden knew what was happening, the ridiculous puppy was nestled in his hands and the seedy-looking man was holding out his palm.

"Here, now!" said Mr. Hilden, startled, "I don't want to buy a——"

"Ozzerwise," the other interrupted, "I got to drown heem."

"You've got to *drown* him?"

"No money to feed. He got to eat, I got to eat—I no eat for week, month!" cried the seedy-looking man in an unexpectedly loud voice, throwing his hands around eloquently. "Wan month I no eat! Wan dollar, plizz."

Mr. Hilden was not proof against the thought of a man who had not eaten for a month, although the statement seemed perhaps a trifle exaggerated; and so, holding the puppy in his left hand, with his right he reached into his pocket and took out a dollar bill. "Here's a dollar, then," he said, "but I can't keep the——"

"God bless you, frand!" shouted the seedy-looking man; and snatching the dollar bill he bolted down the street as if ten starving lions were hot on his heels.

"But the puppy!" Mr. Hilden cried. "You forgot the puppy!"

However, the seedy-looking man was gone.

"Now, how do you like that?" said Mr. Hilden to himself, and regarded the puppy with a puzzled frown.

The puppy wagged its ridiculous tail.

"Hm!" Mr. Hilden said. "Friendly little rascal, aren't you? If that fellow hasn't eaten for a month, I wonder how long it's been since *you* had something?" And with the puppy snuggled comfortably in the crook of his arm, Mr. Hilden returned to the lunchroom.

Here the puppy proved either that it too had not eaten for a month or that it possessed one of the really spectacular appetites of all time, for it consumed so much hamburger that Mr. Hilden began to fear it would burst.

The lunchroom proprietor came to watch this impressive eating performance.

"That's some dog, Mr. Hilden," he said admiringly, "what would you call it? A dachshund? No, I guess it ain't rightly a dachshund at that, something more on the order of—what do they call them bushy dogs? Poodles, is it? But no, I'd say he's more or less a bloodhound, although——" Here he stopped with a puzzled look and then laughed. "Mr. Hilden," he said, "I bet you that's the only dog of its kind in the world. You got yourself something there!"

Having siphoned up the very last crumb of hamburger, the puppy sniffed around to see if there was any more, and concluding that there wasn't, waddled over to Mr. Hilden, lay down and fell asleep, with one chubby paw draped over Mr. Hilden's foot.

"Dog sure likes you, Mr. Hilden!" the lunchroom proprietor exclaimed. "A one-man dog, I guess you'd call him! What's his name?"

Mr. Hilden began to explain that the dog was not really his, that is, he had not intended to buy it and was only taking care of the animal until he could find someone to give it to; but he had hardly begun before he stopped. It was funny, but looking down at the puppy, and hearing those words—"one-man dog"—he felt a little tickly warm sensation. What was it? Why, Mr. Hilden concluded wonderingly, it was pride!

"Or ain't he got a name?" asked the lunchroom proprietor.

Now, if there was one name above all other names that Mr. Hilden admired, it was the middle name of a certain American author whose works had given Mr. Hilden endless pleasure as a child, since they transported the reader to that magic, vanished America of legend—the America of the great mysterious forests, the whispering glades, the noble redman gliding wraithlike on some thrilling mission of vengeance or conquest.

If he and Judith had ever had a son, Mr. Hilden had intended to bestow this beautiful name on the boy. And now, with the lunchroom proprietor's question, it rang in Mr. Hilden's head with all its old glory and splendour.

"Certainly he's got a name," he said firmly. "Fenimore!"

Considerable changes were introduced into Mr. Hilden's life almost at once by Fenimore. The first was the matter of the hotel. A sign in the lobby stated plainly that pets would not be tolerated in any circumstances; Fenimore, therefore, travelled back and forth between Mr. Hilden's room and the outdoor world underneath Mr. Hilden's jacket. But soon it began to seem outrageous to Mr. Hilden that a dog as extra-ordinary and well-behaved as Fenimore should be obliged to lead this furtive, pariah-like existence.

And so he looked around the neighbourhood and found a nice double room with a tiny kitchenette attached in a rooming house where the landlady said she had no objection to a dog, so long as his behaviour was that of a gentleman.

The second change was the attention Mr. Hilden began to attract in the streets.

Few indeed were proof against Fenimore's peculiar charms. His appearance was striking enough; his method of loco-motion, or, to put it more accurately, his style, was equally rare and fascinating. He seemed to proceed as much from side to side as forward; that is to say, while his legs went back and forth in the normal manner, his body swayed sideways in a kind of hammocklike fashion, so that, pausing to investigate tree trunk or hydrant, Fenimore appeared to come to a stop not all in one piece but in instalments. This rhythmic body swing was rounded out, given the final fancy trimmings, by the gentle flapping of Fenimore's long beagleish ears and the graceful movements of his somewhat collie-like tail.

Fenimore coming down the street halted people in their tracks, and he had the effect of leaving good feeling in his wake. It was impossible to look at him without laughing, and a laugh is something that improves the whole world—particularly if the cause of it does not mind, and Fenimore did not. He merely looked up at you with a liquid, friendly eye, wagged his tail, and, you would have sworn, was on the verge of laughing too.

Fenimore was particularly admired by a group of youths who had formed themselves into a baseball team called the Young Giants, who ranged in age from about ten to fourteen. A delegation of Young Giants called on Mr. Hilden one day and asked if he, or Fenimore, would have any objection if they officially appointed Fenimore the mascot of the team? The duties were not onerous, merely requiring Fenimore's attendance at each scheduled Young Giant game; and they assured Mr. Hilden that they would take excellent care of him while he was engaged in mascoting.

Mr. Hilden thought it over. Fenimore's increasing prominence and importance in the world of affairs gave him pleasure and certainly he had no intention of standing in his way. Yet——

"How often do you play?" he asked.

"We got a game scheduled every day for the next month, and maybe all summer," he was told.

"Well," Mr. Hilden said, and hesitated. "I guess it's all right," he began again, "but——"

"Honest, Mr. Hilden, we'd take *good* care of him! Gee, we wouldn't think of letting anything happen to *Fenimore!*"

Hearing his name, Fenimore wagged his tail agreeably.

"Oh, I know you wouldn't," Mr. Hilden assured them hastily. "It's just that——"

But he could not quite come out with it. The truth was, the thought of all those afternoons without Fenimore, when Fenimore would be mascoting, was a depressing one.

Then a superb, simple idea struck Mr. Hilden, and he marvelled that it had not occurred to him at once. "Would you mind very much," he said shyly, "if I come along too?"

So Mr. Hilden had little time for sitting in the park these days. In the morning, after breakfast, he and Fenimore had their walk to take, a long, leisurely perambulation, with many halts and pauses, not only for Fenimore's attention to necessary dog etiquette, but because people were always asking about him and patting his head and generally admiring him, after having had their laugh.

Then there was lunch and a short nap, and then the big affair of the day, when Mr. Hilden and Fenimore would repair to the neighbourhood playground and take up their official positions—or rather Fenimore's official position—as mascot of the Young Giants, seated midway on the players' bench.

Here the effect of Fenimore was equally beneficent. He appeared to understand very soon that mighty and important matters were taking place, for his deportment could not have been improved upon. His attitude was composed but watchful, and he raised his voice only when the voices of the Young Giants were raised either in triumph or in protest.

Perhaps it was this feeling of genuine and sympathetic support that flowed from Fenimore, perhaps it was simply his appearance on the bench—in any event the batting and fielding averages of the Young Giants began to improve, and their teamwork became a pleasure to behold.

But now came the biggest change of all.

"My, Mr. Hilden," a soft old voice said behind him as he waited with Fenimore for the traffic light to change, "that's a wonderful dog you got. I been meaning to tell you for a long time how much I think you deserve compliments for owning such a dog."

This was no new experience for Mr. Hilden, but it gratified him none the less. "Thank you," he said, turning to see who this latest admirer of Fenimore was. A small lady of approximately his own years, she stooped and patted Fenimore gently on his head. "I don't think I know your name?" Mr. Hilden said doubtfully. "And yet the face is familiar."

"We lived a few doors away when you and Mrs. Hilden were in the Belmore," the small lady with the soft voice explained. "Mrs. Hilden and I used to meet each morning almost in Groschen's Market. Mr. Arberman, my husband, he was alive then too. You wouldn't remember me, Mr. Hilden, but you used to buy candy for my daughter Ruthie—a grown woman she is now, that's how time flies, as they say."

"Why, certainly I remember Ruthie," Mr. Hilden said, "and you too, Mrs. Arberman. I knew the face was familiar. And where are you living now?"

"With Ruthie still, Mr. Hilden. The same place."

"Ruthie's not married, then?"

Mrs. Arberman made an expressive gesture. "It's on, it's off—it's almost, but never all the way. But next week she's going up in the mountains for the whole month, and there's a certain fellow—well, she has high hopes."

"And you never married again, Mrs. Arberman?"

Mrs. Arberman gave a little laugh. "And who'd want an old woman like me?"

"Old?" said Mr. Hilden gallantly. "Why, I should say not! I told you the face was familiar when I saw you. That's how little you've changed."

"That's very lovely of you, Mr. Hilden," Mrs. Arberman said with the same little laugh that seemed somehow to end in a sigh, "but it isn't true. It's true I feel young inside, younger even than I was when Ruthie was born, but—— Well, all the time Ruthie and others keep saying, Now, Ma, act your age, until I can't get away from it, I'm old and I should just be sitting on the benches in the park with all the others. Just like you were doing, Mr. Hilden, do you know that?—until you got your dog. My, what a change in you there was then!"

"I know it," said Mr. Hilden. "Getting Fenimore was the luckiest thing in my life, except the day I met Judith."

"Something like that I wish could happen to me," Mrs. Arberman said. "A dog or something to come into my life. What's his name, Mr. Hilden?"

"Fenimore," Mr. Hilden said proudly.

"A beautiful name! Did you think of it all by yourself, Mr. Hilden?"

Mr. Hilden explained how Fenimore had happened to come by his distinguished name. "But now, Mrs. Arberman," he continued, "your saying you wish something like Fenimore could come into your life because you are maybe a little down in the dumps—now, do you know what my Judith would always say when she was feeling a little blue? 'Maurice,' she would say, 'there's one wonderful thing about being a woman, which is that she has always got a sure cure for the glooms'— that's what my Judith would call the blues, the glooms. 'Always, Maurice,' she would say, 'always she can go out and buy herself a new hat.' And that is just what Judith would do, and," Mr. Hilden concluded, "if you take my advice, why don't you just stop off somewhere this afternoon and see what a new hat will do for you?"

Mrs. Arberman went a little pink.

"Excuse me, Mrs. Arberman, if I've offended you," Mr. Hilden said hastily.

"You haven't at all!" she protested. "And maybe that is exactly what I need. Mr. Hilden, thank you for the suggestion. How long it's been since I bought a new hat, now that you mention it! I've almost forgotten what it's like! My," she said, chuckling, "when Ruthie comes home to-night and sees me all dressed up in a new hat, won't she be surprised!"

But Ruthie did not see her mother in a new hat that evening.

It was not that Mrs. Arberman had not been able to find a hat that pleased her. The very opposite was the case. For she had acted on Mr. Hilden's suggestion and gone in to Mme. Dolores' Hat Shoppe on the Concourse to look around. And almost at once she had seen it, The Hat, positively a master-piece of a hat, a hat that had caused Mrs. Arberman's heart to beat faster than it had for years.

It was a purple hat, in shape somewhat like one of the boats men push around with long sticks in Italy, while singing, but its most graceful and endearing feature was the feather that sprouted out from the top, yet not altogether from the top, somewhat from the side, slightly on the bias, as you might say. This feather was purple too, but of an even richer hue.

"So?" Mme. Dolores said genially, coming up to Mrs. Arberman. "Have you anything special in mind, moddim?"

"That hat," Mrs. Arberman said, pointing to the purple treasure. "Could I try it on?"

"Moddim has excellent taste," Mme. Dolores applauded. With one elegant gesture she conducted Mrs. Arberman to a seat before a three-sided mirror, then plucked the purple hat from its roost, and gave it to Mrs. Arberman.

Mrs. Arberman looked into the mirror eagerly—and her heart, that had been beating so gaily, took a sickening plunge.

No, it was not the hat. The hat was as beautiful and desirable as ever. The trouble was the face underneath the hat. The hat and the face simply did not go together.

Mrs. Arberman shook her head, and without saying a word, as if she understood perfectly, Mme. Dolores swiftly removed the lovely hat.

"Now, we have something very nice over here," she said in a brisk, cheerful voice, and produced an altogether different kind of hat, a gloomy affair that looked like something a general or admiral might wear at a funeral. Others followed, equally depressing.

"I guess not to-day, thank you," Mrs. Arberman said apologetically. But she could not leave before glancing once more at the purple hat with the feather standing proudly and gracefully overhead.

She went back to the apartment and sat down. Maybe Ruthie was right after all. According to Ruthie she should stay at home more, not walk around everywhere as she liked to, looking at people and listening to all the million and one things that were going on. That was not the proper behaviour for elderly ladies, Ruthie said—they should sit in the living-room and knit or read a nice book. Yes, perhaps Ruthie was right. For in the mirror at Mme. Dolores's Mrs. Arberman had seen a bright, challenging, youthful hat—and an old worn face beneath it.

An *old* face.

Yet, as she had said to Mr. Hilden, she simply did not feel old. She did not want to sit in the living-room and knit or read a quiet, elevating book. She wanted to get out and live some more; she didn't want to park here with one foot in the grave and the other trying to get into it too.

"That hat was made for me," Mrs. Arberman said to herself. "It just *is* me. The *hat* is me but the face isn't. So—so——"

So what?

Go on, do something about it! a voice said within her. Look at Mr. Hilden! See the difference that's come over him since he got that nice dog Fenimore! Why, he looks and acts ten years younger, not pining away for the grave any more, like he was before! Do something, Molly!

Mrs. Arberman went to the mirror in the bathroom and examined her face. She stroked her fingers over the heavy clusters of wrinkles around the eyes, and pressed back the sagging cheeks. That was what had made the beautiful purple hat seem impossible for her, those wrinkles and the soft sagging flesh.

Then an extraordinary idea struck Mrs. Arberman. At first she had to take her courage in both hands to examine it; but then she reflected, can it hurt just to talk about it?

She went to the telephone and called various people and wrote down several names and addresses. And that was how it happened that Ruthie Arberman, coming home a little later, heard her mother making an appointment to go to a doctor's office for a consultation.

"A consultation with a doctor, Mother?" Ruthie said. "What kind of doctor? What's wrong with you?"

"A plastic surgeon," Mrs. Arberman said.

"A plastic surgeon! But why?" Ruthie cried.

"Why, what do you think, Ruthie?" said Mrs. Arberman, as coolly and calmly as you please. "To talk about having my face fixed, of course!"

Some six weeks after this conversation, Mrs. Arberman came by to see me, as she had promised me she would. By then we were good friends. I had learned all about Ruthie and Mr. Hilden and Mr. Hilden's dog Fenimore and the purple hat and had told Mrs. Arberman that no, I did not believe she was entering her second childhood, as Ruthie maintained. She simply had the desire to become young again and not to sit back on a park bench and doze in the sun but to do something about it.

So, while Ruthie had gone off for her month in the mountains, Mrs. Arberman had entered the hospital and the wrinkles and sagging flesh had been removed from her face.

And now here Mrs. Arberman was in my office, looking at me inquiringly.

"You like it, Doctor?"

"Beautiful," I said.

We referred to the hat. For having made her decision, Mrs. Arberman had gone back to Mme. Dolores and put a deposit on the hat, to be held until after the operation had been performed and she had left the hospital, to see if she would then feel qualified to wear it.

"But it's not only the hat, Mrs. Arberman," I said. "Isn't that a complete new outfit you're wearing?"

Mrs. Arberman nodded her head. "To-day, it's quite an

occasion," she explained. "You see, Doctor, Mr. Hilden—Mr. Hilden has become an umpire."

"An umpire!"

She nodded again. "For the Young Giants. Instead of just sitting on the players' bench he wanted to be doing something, like Fenimore—Fenimore was mascoting and Mr. Hilden wanted to be active too. So he suggested it and everyone said it was just what they wanted, a real expert umpire.

"Yesterday I saw him umpiring for the first time," Mrs. Arberman went on enthusiastically. "Oh, Doctor, it was fine! The boys, they argue sometimes, you know, the Young Giants and the Junior Yankees, that was the name of the team they happened to be playing: 'You're out!' 'I am not out!' 'You are too out!' 'I am not either out!' and things like this. And Mr. Hilden, he just comes up quietly and dignified and holds up his hand and says like a judge, '*You are out.*' And that is all there is to it. It was so fine," Mrs. Arberman explained, "I applauded and applauded."

"And what's the big occasion to-day?" I asked.

"The first game of the Junior World's Series," Mrs. Arberman told me. "And after Mr. Hilden has finished umpiring, we are stopping over on the Concourse for a bite to eat with Fenimore—and—guess who, Doctor?"

"Who?"

"Ruthie too!"

"Ruthie too!" I exclaimed. "Then she's back? And she's seen you?"

"She's back and she's seen me, and, Doctor"—Mrs. Arberman here took a delicate lace-trimmed handkerchief from her bag—"do you know what she said when she saw me, coming in like she did yesterday, and I was sitting in the living-room waiting for her, but with my back towards her, and knitting?"

"You were knitting, Mrs. Arberman?"

"I planned it just like that, Doctor.

" 'Well, Mother,' Ruthie said, 'I'm glad to see you've come to your senses while I've been away.' She meant that I was sitting at home knitting, you see.

" 'Yes, Ruthie, I have,' I said, very quietly, and I turned around and looked at her.

"And Ruthie stared at me and stared at me and stared at me, and she dropped her bag to the floor with a bang—and, Doctor, you could have knocked me over with a feather, because then Ruthie put out her arms and cried 'Mother! Why, Mother—I *like* it!' And then there we were, the two of us, laughing like fools together."

And remembering the scene, Mrs. Arberman laughed again, so heartily that the purple hat became somewhat displaced.

"But I must be going," she said. "Mr. Hilden will be waiting for me, and between the two of us, Doctor, I think maybe —he just *maybe* has intentions." She felt the purple hat. "So," she said, smiling, "where is the mirror, please?"

The Doll That Talked

ANYONE SEEING FRANK GORDON IN MY CONSULTATION ROOM would have granted that here was a man who had had more than his share of suffering. Frank's face was marred by a broken nose, giving him a comic, grotesque look, like a sad clown. But he carried a far worse burden: he lived in the dead world of the deaf mute.

And so I expected to find a dull resignation in his eyes. I couldn't have been more wrong. Frank Gordon's blue eyes were glowing and young and cheerful.

There was still another surprise in his record. The accident in which he had broken his nose had happened some ten years before, when he had missed his footing in the dark and fallen down a flight of stairs. And yet although the broken nose interfered seriously with his breathing, he had waited all those years before coming to a doctor to have it fixed. Why?

The answer lay in a recent experience. By and by Frank told me the story—or, I should say, wrote it down for me in his quick, graceful hand.

*   *   *

Frank Gordon hadn't been born a deaf mute. Up to the age of four he had been a perfectly normal youngster, talking a blue streak, full of questions, as mischievous and lively as a monkey.

Then one evening as he was being tucked into bed he complained, "Mama, my throat hurts. Bring me a glass of water, please?" After getting him the water, Mrs. Gordon felt the

171

little boy's forehead. There didn't seem to be any fever and she thought that by morning the sore throat would be gone and forgotten.

The next day Frank was somewhat listless and complained again about his throat. Mrs. Gordon decided that it was a cold coming on and kept him in the house all day. The following day was the same, and the next day too. And then, disdaining further concealment, the enemy showed itself for what it was. When the family doctor arrived, he was greeted by a very grim situation indeed.

Diphtheria will declare itself in one of two ways, either dramatically, with high temperatures and severe headaches, or, as in Frank Gordon's case, with a slow, seemingly innocuous build-up. By the time the disease was diagnosed, most of the damage had been done to Frank, and it was nip and tuck whether he could be pulled through at all. Thanks to his sturdy constitution and Mrs. Gordon's devoted care, he won the desperate struggle—but the disease had destroyed his hearing and scarred his throat so badly that he could not speak.

At first puzzled and uncomprehending, Frank's blue eyes slowly became bitter as he understood the terrible thing that had happened to him. He would wake up morning after morning thinking that now, in the light of day, the bad dream would be over—but of course it never was. His family lavished care and attention on him, but Frank's bitterness and sense of betrayal only increased. At the New York School for the Deaf, where he was sent, he could never get himself to join in with the others. The one question blotted out everything else—Why? Why did this have to happen?

His family and their friends and relatives thought long and hard about Frank's future. The School for the Deaf helped too in suggesting possible jobs, as it helps all its graduates. Frank tried his hand at half a dozen trades but couldn't last in any one of them for more than a week. He was conscious of the curiosity and inquisitive, pitying glances of those around him; and added to his bitterness was a growing sense of self-pity.

Then Frank picked out a job for himself. At the time it gave him a certain perverse pleasure. Surely this was the right place for him—in a world of little creatures as silent and un-hearing as he!

The job he picked out was in a doll factory.

With his long, agile fingers, Frank soon became adept at putting the final delicate touches to each day's quota of rosy-faced dolls, and he was regarded as one of the company's most valuable employees. But he remained as solitary as ever in his silent world. He turned away from the friendly advances made by the others in the doll factory and stayed at home on the day of the annual company outing.

Probably he was what is called "accident-prone." At any rate when he slipped on the stairs and broke his nose he was almost glad. Here was another reason to feel sorry for him-self. He would not think of having the broken nose repaired. It gave him pleasure to suffer.

Then one spring day Frank Gordon—now a young man in his middle twenties—noticed a change in the neighbourhood.

Down the block lived the Caulder family, husband, wife, and five-year-old daughter Carol. Carol was always racing up and down the block on her scooter, a freckled, charming child, thoroughly secure in the world of affection her young parents gave her. She had tried often to talk with Frank as he trudged home in the evenings but, getting no reply, had asked her mother "why Mr. Gordon never talks." After she had heard that he could never talk, she would gaze at him with silent pity.

This Tuesday evening Frank became aware that Carol wasn't playing on the sidewalk as usual. Getting home, he asked his sister in a written note: "What's happened to Carol Caulder?"

His sister pronounced the answer slowly and Frank read her lips.

"Diphtheria."

But Carol's case was different. Hers had the violent onset—aching throat and high temperature—that left the doctor in no doubt as to the identity of the disease. He administered the saving anti-toxin at once and the deadly, greyish-green web that had begun to form over throat and tonsils was cleared away as if by magic.

But though Frank's and Carol's cases were so dissimilar, the remarkable thing was that the end effect seemed to be precisely the same.

Carol too seemed to have been turned into a deaf mute.

The doctor assured her distraught father and mother that this could only be temporary. There was no evidence of permanent physical damage; the throat had not been scarred and the hearing mechanism was intact. But in spite of everything that the doctor and Mr. and Mrs. Caulder could think of to do, silent day followed silent day. The little girl simply would not speak.

The doctor confessed that he was stumped.

But, learning all this, Frank Gordon wasn't stumped. He was sure he knew exactly what had happened. Carol felt, just as he had felt, that her parents—her safe, secure world—had somehow betrayed her. The disease had attacked her with all its savagery right from the beginning. To her, this seemed to mean that at any moment, without warning, the sunny world could become a nightmare. At any moment her parents could change from two loving, all-powerful people into two strangers who just let you suffer, who did not use their power to drive your pain away.

Her answer—one might say her revenge—was to turn her back on this puzzling, cruel world and retreat into dead silence.

Frank knew that the only cure was to persuade Carol to

come out of that shell of silence and rejoin the world. Only in that way would she be able to adjust herself to her experience.

Somehow, she must be made to speak.

But how?

Never before had Frank Gordon been concerned about another human being. He had always been too busy feeling sorry for himself. But he *knew* what was going on in Carol's mind and he wished to help her. So that night, for the first time in his life, he prayed. He asked in his prayer to be shown how to persuade Carol to speak.

He went to bed and fell asleep. By and by, he had a dream. In the dream, he saw himself at work at his bench in the doll factory. He was working on a beautiful doll, the most beautiful doll he had ever seen. And somehow he knew that the doll was to be a present for Carol.

Then was that the answer to his prayer? To give Carol a doll he had made all by himself?

Surely, it seemed too easy! And however could a doll make her talk?

But the dream had been so clear that the next day Frank asked for and received permission from his employer to make a very, very special doll for a little sick girl. And probably never before had such care been taken with a doll. It was a beauty.

When he had finished the doll, Frank inspected it, and thought:

Please make Carol talk! Just a few words—just two or three words—but please, *make her talk!*

After work that afternoon he tucked the beautiful doll in a bright red-ribboned package under his arm and went to the Caulders' apartment. When Mrs. Caulder came to the door he gave her the package. A note was attached to the ribbon. *For Carol*, it said.

Frank saw her smile and read the words of thanks on her

lips and somehow felt better than he had ever since he could remember.

But that night, he became doubtful again. Carol had been given all sorts of presents during her sickness. She had turned away from all of them—the dolls and everything else—with the same dull, uncaring eyes.

How could his doll be any different? Yet the dream had been so clear!

In the middle of the night the telephone rang in the Gordons' apartment. Frank's sister answered it. An excited voice came over the wire. The voice was so excited that for a minute or two Frank's sister had difficulty in recognizing it as Mrs. Caulder's.

Mrs. Caulder seemed to be laughing and crying at the same time. She had an extraordinary story to tell.

That afternoon, she had given Carol Frank's doll and explained from whom the present had come. Carol had looked at the doll dully and pushed it off her bed to the floor. Close to despair, the parents had sat through their tasteless dinner and gone to bed early.

A few hours later Mrs. Calder had felt a small hand on her arm. Startled, she had turned on the bedside light. Carol stood there. For the first time in weeks the mother heard her daughter's voice again.

"Mama," Carol said, "may I have a glass of water?"

"Darling, darling!" Mrs. Caulder cried. "Of course you may! A glass of water—milk—anything, anything you want!"

"It's not for me," Carol explained. "It's for the doll Mr. Frank brought me. She woke me up just now to tell me. I guess," Carol said slowly, "I guess she must be feeling sick like I did a while ago. She said her throat hurt. She asked me to get her a glass of water to make it feel better."

One may or may not accept Carol's assurance that the doll *did* talk—but seeing Frank Gordon's bright, cheerful eyes I knew beyond all doubt that his prayer had been answered. And doubly answered! For not only did Carol leave her self-imposed prison and come back and join the world again—also, Frank saw suddenly that his life had not been without meaning after all. To-day, he believes that everything that happened to him had a purpose behind it. He feels that he has been of some value, some use. He looks forward to a new life, to be lived to the full.

And I felt confident that he would have it, because of his compassion for another human being—which turned him from an old young man into a young and happy one.

Two Lives in One

E VERY YEAR IT ARRIVED AT THE SAME TIME, THE SAME LETTER —the same, that is, except for the year:

Dear Classmate:
Don't forget the annual dinner of the P & S Alumni Association. As far as our class is concerned, it marks our thirtieth year since graduation from Charley's Emporium. BE THERE. It will be good to see you and the others again.

Best regards,
Class Secretary

Every year, like a faithful son of the College of Physicians and Surgeons of Columbia University, I had meant to respond to the letter. I had put it in a conspicuous place on my desk and I had marked the desk calendar with a red cross on the proper date. But every year something had seemed to come up at the last moment to prevent me from going.

This year I went through the same routine: put the letter in the prominent place, marked the calendar with a bigger cross than ever. However, this time, for a change, nothing had cropped up at the last minute. So now I had no excuse. If I did not attend the thirtieth reunion, I would never be able to look myself in the eye again.

I would *be there.*

And now that there was no getting out of it, I found that I was looking forward to the evening. Think of it—thirty years, a whole generation, since we had slung our coats and hats across to Old Charley, the coatroom attendant!

Old Charley. . . . It sent a warm rush of affection over me to think of him again.

For it was old Charley who had rescued me from my worst failing at P & S, the terrible time I had always had when called on in the pathology classroom. I felt sure I was doomed to flunk, for no matter how faithfully I had prepared myself, the information requested by the pathology prof. would fly out of my head the moment I rose to my feet. The why and wherefore of this mystery, God only knew; I didn't.

"Say, Max," said old Charley one winter afternoon as he handed me my coat and hat, "there's something I been wondering about that a friend of mine was asking—since he knows where I work, he figures I can find out anything I want to know about doctors and medicine and such. Maybe you wouldn't mind telling me?"

"If I can," I said gloomily, for my hide still stung from my latest horrible failure in the pathology classroom.

"It's just this," Charley said. "How do you know a person has pneumonia? Can you tell me?"

"Sure," I said, and took a deep breath. "To begin with— well, pneumonia is an infectious disease of the lungs, divided into several stages. The first stage is the stage of engorgement, where the capillaries of the alveolar walls are dilated with blood. The second stage is the stage of red hepatization."

"Red what?" said Charley.

"Hepatization. That's when an abundant inflammatory exudate fills the alveoli and clots; it consists of a coarse-meshed network of fibrin in which are entangled numerous pneumococci, red corpuscles, polymorphonuclear leucocytes and some desquamated epithelial cells."

"Epi?" Charley said faintly.

"Epithelial cells. The next stage is the stage of *grey* hepatization, which from a microscopical viewpoint is the degenerated condition of the cells of the exudate. The leucocytes have lost their clear outline and have become granular, but still show evidence of phagocytic activity."

"Phago who?" Charley said.

"Phagocytic activity. Desquamated epithelium are more abundant. The next stage is the stage of resolution and healing, which consists of the relining of the alveoli with alveolar epithelium after the complete removal of the exudate."

"Listen," Charley said, "all I wanted to know was how can you tell if a person has pneumonia?"

"Well," I said, "now you know."

"I guess I do. Question is," said Charley, "why couldn't you tell *him* that?"

"Tell who?"

"Old Dinwiddie. Ain't he your prof. in pathology?"

Old Dinwiddie was indeed my pathology professor, an enormous, craggy, irascible Scot. Only a couple of days ago Professor Dinwiddie had invited me to refresh his ears with the very same information I had now so fluently delivered to Charley; and I had mumbled and stammered along until finally Dinwiddie had proclaimed me to be "a hopeless eegnoramus."

"Yes," I said to Charley, puzzled by this mystery, "it's old Dinwiddie all right, and what you say is true. Somehow or other I wasn't able to tell him a darned thing when he asked me about pneumonia."

"I'll tell *you* something," Charley said, leaning confidentially towards me across the coatroom counter. "You've got a special kind of feeling about Professor Dinwiddie. He scares you stiff. Just the look of him paralyses you. Well, now, Max, my boy, I want to tell you something *in confidence*. At the last Faculty Ball Professor Dinwiddie had a mite too much to drink and somehow or other got mixed up between the ladies' and the gents' retiring room. Didn't find it out, though, till he was *in* there. Then, when he heard ladies approaching, all he could do was jump into one of the little booths and lock the door. In consequence of which he spent the whole evening in solitary confinement, afraid to come out. How do I know this?" Charley asked triumphantly. "Because it was me who let him out, closing up as I was when everybody—I mean everybody except old Dinwiddie—had gone home. Swore I'd never tell no one about it, but seems to me from what I hear the condition you're in requires emergency measures.

"So," said Charley finally, "the next time old Dinwiddie asks you to stand up and tell him what this is or what that is, don't you look at him like he's standing there in front of you with those eyes of his blazing at you. Instead you think of him the way he *was*, like I told you. There he was, that night, sitting in that little booth for four long hours, with those big feet of his tucked up underneath, sweating blood for fear one of the ladies would get curious as to why the door of the booth was closed yet there wasn't any *feet* showing on the floor underneath the door—and would peek under the door and find out."

Never thereafter was I able to regard Professor Dinwiddie with awe; now I felt only a pleasant sense of sympathy and gratitude, gratitude for the wonderful laugh the story had given me. Pathological information came bursting from me at his slightest request, and I was taken into the good man's favour.

"I can see ye've changed your ways," he said approvingly. "You're putting in your time studying now instead of fashing about with foolishness. I give ye credit for it and retract what I said about ye."

I dressed myself with great care for the class reunion and at the appointed time presented myself at the appointed place. The cocktail lounge adjoining the dining-room where the reunion dinner was to be held was crowded with people, swirling in smoke and talk. I roamed here and there, seeking for familiar faces but could find none—if members of my class were there, then they had changed beyond recognition.

At last, however, I spotted someone I knew. He had hardly changed at all in those thirty years—hardly at all! And I grinned at him and he grinned back. Who was it? Me. I had just seen myself in one of the mirrors on the walls.

Slowly the crowd trickled off into the dining-room and I found my way to table #14, the table for the class of 1923. And as I came up to it, a well-remembered voice rang out in greeting:

"My God, Max, is that *you*? What's happened to you? How you've changed!"

So with a bang I returned to earth.

And how all the rest of them had changed too.

But if I closed my eyes and just listened to their voices, they were the same. Barney Auer was the same—confident, glowing—and Mickey Henry's deep, pleasant voice hadn't altered at all. And as for Mary James—she not only sounded the same, she looked as beautiful as ever. She was a successful doctor, too, in spite of that gloomy prediction back in 1923.

Up on a dais at the end of the great room were the special guests of the evening. And good Lord!—was I seeing things? Who was that in the place of honour? I rubbed my eyes and had another look, but he was still there and his face was still very much the same as I remembered it.

I leaned over to Mary. "Who's that up there? Is it really who it seems to be?"

"Of course it is," she smiled. "Didn't you know? He's the guest of honour to-night—old Charley, Charley of the coatroom."

"But he must be—why, he was ancient when *we* were there, and that's thirty years ago!"

"He's eighty-six," she informed me. "Doesn't look it, does he?"

Indeed, he didn't. Here, being honoured for his fifty and more years of faithful service—here was a man who had hardly changed from the good friend and adviser I remembered.

"I wonder what his secret is?" I murmured.

"I think that's simple to answer," Mary told me. "Did he ever do anything to help you, Max?"

"Did he!" I said warmly. "If it hadn't been for him, I would have flunked pathology, that's all."

"He gave me a lift when I needed one too," Mary said. "In fact I think you'd find he helped just about every one of us in one way or another. He looked on each new class coming to P & S as his boys and girls—not that he'd ever say anything sentimental like that, of course. But he made it his business to find out all he could about how we were getting along, and naturally he knew all the professors' characteristics and their strong points and weak points, and so if anything was going wrong he was able to give you a pretty good tip about how to correct it. In a way, he lived his life in ours."

Marvelling at the old man, I felt sure Mary had diagnosed the secret of his youthfulness correctly. Every year he had started all over again, not looking at the new batch of students with tired bored cynicism but instead as if he, the old coatroom attendant, were taking the first step on the hard, perilous and thrilling road to becoming a doctor, to learn with us, to rejoice with us in our moments of triumph, and to comfort us and show us the way out when we became downhearted.

Well, that was Charley's secret. Now, what about Boysie's?

Boysie—Professor James Boysland—was the man I remembered best of all for his skill as a surgeon. Now Boysie sat at the table of the class of 1903. There were not many left now, fifty years after they had gone forth to storm the citadels; their shoulders were bent, the old heads were bald or white —except for Boysie's. Boysie could still boast a pepper and salt mixture, and more pepper than salt; and his eyes were not yet yellowed and rheumy, and he sat there as sturdily upright as a youngster. So it was obvious that Boysie had a secret of youth too.

By and by, after the more or less official part of the evening was over, people began to mix around; several of the old gentlemen at Boysie's table left, but not he. I went over to him and cleared my throat to attract his attention. He looked up at me with those clear blue-grey eyes of his and said, "Young Maltz! Sit down and tell me what you've been doing with yourself."

"Young" Maltz sat down, as grateful for the adjective as for the invitation. "I don't deserve that description as much as you do," I said. "How have you managed it—staying so young?"

Boysie offered me a cigar, lit his own, and took a sip from his brandy glass. "Well, now," he said, "after those flattering words—what would you say if I told you that you see before you something of a Dr. Jekyll and a Mr. Hyde? That is, a man who is living two lives in one?"

"I'd want to know all about it," I said.

"As a matter of fact," Boysie went on in the same gravely humorous tone, so that I began to suspect he was having a private joke at my expense (as he had been known to do thirty years ago), "as a matter of fact, I consider mine to be a case far more remarkable than that of the unfortunate Jekyll and the horrible Mr. Hyde. For what was that, after all?— chemical mumbo-jumbo. Whereas my prescription doesn't require any drugs—and lets me enjoy the pleasures of the mature while guaranteeing at the same time a palate unjaded by age."

Then Boysie took another good sip of his brandy and a puff from his cigar as if to point up what he was saying.

"Remarkable, sir," I said, in something of the same tone.

Boysie lifted his bushy eyebrows at me, and then chuckled. "No, it isn't a joke," he continued. "As some young people say to-day, I am levelling with you, my dear fellow. And here is something that will back me up." As he said this he took a small object from his pocket and put it on the table in front of me.

It was the tiny, dainty figurine of a dancing girl, carved in wood. Raised on tiptoe, arms outflung, head tossed back, it seemed to glow with the very spirit of youth.

"Like it?" asked Boysie.

"Very much. Who did it?"

"A young fellow I know—a protégé, you might say."

"Very gifted, I think," I said.

"Glad you think so," said Boysie. "I'll tell you the sculptor's story." And leaning back in his chair and blowing out another fragrant cloud of smoke, he began the following account:

During the war years, with the acute shortage of doctors, Boysie had doubled and tripled his regular load of work by serving wherever he could, wherever the need was greatest. He piled upon himself more than most people could bear until it seemed that even he must crumple unless he found some sort of release. The nights were the worst time; racked by the unending tension, he could sleep only fitfully.

One evening, on leaving the hospital where he had been operating, he heard the wail of a baby in the delivery room nearby.

"For some reason I found myself musing about that child," Boysie continued. "Was it a boy or a girl, I wondered? What was the colour of its eyes? How much had it weighed at

186

birth? And what was going to happen to it, years and years from now? What adventures lay ahead?

"Making a little game of it, I decided that the baby was a boy with dark hair and bluish-grey eyes. I further decided that he'd grow into a lanky youngster, a great one for patching up maimed household pets and disabled birds. When the usual childhood diseases came along, he'd be fascinated by the whole business of diagnosis and treatment, so that in every case he was almost sorry when the illness was over and he had to go back to the prosaic business of being healthy again.

"When he was twelve, it was obvious to the whole family that he had been cut out to be a doctor from the very beginning."

Boysie raised his eyebrows again whimsically.

"But there I pulled myself up short. I suddenly realized who he was, this imaginary child I'd created. Who else but myself!

"Then I began to think about that twelve-year-old me; and I tell you, I envied him heartily. If only I could change places with him and experience again the long, slow, wonderful uphill climb of his next dozen years, learning to be a doctor!

"If by some miracle I could change places for a few hours this evening with my twelve-year-old self, what would I be doing? Studying something or other—perhaps my book of elementary biology.

"I had kept that precious book, and at home I took it down from the shelf and opened it for the first time in forty-odd years. But of course the old spell it used to have for me was gone. There was the trouble with trying to live the past over again. How could I imagine I was that boy once more, turning the pages of his book with breathless excitement to find out what came next, when I *knew* what came next—in his book and in his career?

"And then a great idea struck me.

"Twelve-year-old Boysie had already made up his mind to be a doctor. Let's say he hadn't. Let's imagine he had decided to follow a different line. Let's imagine that in those quiet after-dinner hours he studied not his elementary biology but instead—well, what?"

Boysie puffed on his cigar for a minute or two.

"I want to tell you, I argued with myself back and forth over that, and the more I argued the more important it came to seem. I mean after all you don't just decide what you're going to be in a flash—damn it, it's as important as getting married! So I made up a list for that young twelve-year-old Boysie, his likes and dislikes, his natural facilities—leaving out medicine, naturally.

"When I got through, there it was, staring at me. Twelve-year-old Boysie had a reasonable artistic bent, a good eye, strong wrists and hands, and liked to make sketches of faces and figures. And so——"

And here Boysie nodded at the figurine on the table.

"And so he became a sculptor."

As I thought about what Boysie had said, it seemed to me that he had simply taken a rather roundabout way to a hobby. But it was more than that, I realized. Anyone can choose a hobby and toss it aside, but you don't just throw over a career you've decided to make your life's work. And Boysie didn't quit; he kept at his sculpting night after night, in his "second life."

And soon he found he no longer dreaded bedtime. The nights of fitful tossing were gone; "Young" Boysie's work left him healthily tired. What if "Old" Boysie had had a bad day? There was "Young" Boysie's steady, if slow, advance to cheer him up. The two of them seemed to nod and clasp hands across the years.

"As a doctor, as a professor of advanced age," said Boysie, "I am entitled to my brandy and cigar. As a sculptor of—